HSL:

HEAVEN AS A
SECOND LANGUAGE

BECAUSE TRUTH BECOMES A LIE
IF MEANINGS ARE WRONG

HSL:

HEAVEN AS A
SECOND LANGUAGE

BECAUSE TRUTH BECOMES A LIE
IF MEANINGS ARE WRONG

by
TRICIA KAYE EXMAN

HSL: HEAVEN AS A SECOND LANGUAGE

Scripture quotations are taken from:

Scripture quotations marked NASB are taken from HOLY BIBLE, NEW AMERICAN STANDARD BIBLE, Copyright © 1960, 1962, 1963, 1968, 1971, 1972, 1973, 1975, 1977, 1995 by The Lockman Foundation.

Scripture quotations marked AMPC are taken from the HOLY BIBLE, CLASSIC AMPLIFIED VERSION, Copyright © 1954, 1958, 1962, 1964, 1965, 1987 by The Lockman Foundation.

Scripture quotations marked KJV are taken from The Authorized (King James) Version. Rights in the Authorized Version in the United Kingdom are vested in the Crown. Reproduced by permission of the Crown's patentee, Cambridge University Press

The One New Man Bible, Copyright © 2011 by Rev. William J Morford, True Potential Publishing, Inc.

DEDICATION

To the Ever-present Guide and Counsel who clarifies, adjusts, hones, deepens, and tweaks my understanding, pointing out the broad 'brush stroke' patterns and the 'magnifying glass' details. Without You, I would not attain to all the wealth that comes with the full assurance of understanding of all the hidden treasures of wisdom and knowledge hidden in Christ Jesus (Colossians 2:2-3).

> 1 Corinthians 2:12-15 (NASB): *Now we have received, not the spirit of the world, but the Spirit who is from God, so that we may know the things freely given to us by God, which things we also speak, not in words taught by human wisdom, but in those taught by the Spirit, combining spiritual thoughts with spiritual words.*
>
> *But a natural man does not accept the things of the Spirit of God, for they are foolishness to him; and he cannot understand them, because they are spiritually appraised. But he who is spiritual appraises all things, yet he himself is appraised by no one.*

TABLE OF CONTENTS

READ THIS FIRST

To say 'Thank You' for buying my book, I would like to give you the "Growing & Maturing in I-D-E-N-T-I-T-Y" Podcast 100% FREE!

DOWNLOAD THE PODCAST FREE!

Go To:

www.ThePresenceCoach.com/Free-Podcast

INTRODUCTION

By 2014, I had been earnestly seeking and following the Lord for seven years. It was very apparent to me that I didn't understand His 'language.' I recognized the words He spoke to me, but the meaning I gave to what He was speaking often required a course correction from Him. Listen to Jesus speak to His disciples in Mark 4:24 (AMPC):

> *And He said to them, Be careful what you are hearing. The measure [of thought and study] you give [to the truth you hear] will be the measure [of virtue and knowledge] that comes back to you—and more [besides] will be given to you who hear.*

In any conversation, there are three things we can listen to: what was said, what we heard, or what was meant. One early experience I had of my mind reading what it had been taught instead of what was actually written is in regard to Jesus telling his disciples to buy swords before He heads to Gesthemane after their final meal together. There's a nugget in there that has been glossed over in everything I've ever heard taught, and it is the fundamental key to Jesus' instruction. He never intended the swords to be used. This is clear when he admonishes Peter for using one to cut the right ear off the high priest's servant. Jesus tells Peter to put the sword away with the clear 'rule' that if you live by the sword you will die by the sword. He goes on to heal the servant's ear. The sword Jesus came to bring is the sword of the Spirit (the Holy Spirit that would be poured out). The Holy Spirit will disrupt the peace of our soul as it brings necessary division between it and spirit. This is the battle. So, let's look at this exchange between Jesus and His disciples and see what we've missed.

Luke 22:36-38 (NASB): *And He said to them, "But now, whoever has a money belt is to take it along, likewise also a bag, and whoever has no sword is to sell his coat and buy one. For I tell you that this which is written must be fulfilled in Me, 'AND HE WAS NUMBERED WITH TRANSGRESSORS'; for that which refers to Me has its fulfillment." They said, "Lord, look, here are two swords." And He said to them, "It is enough."*

Did you catch the motivation? Jesus' sole reason for His instruction was because Old Testament prophecy declared the Messiah would be 'numbered with transgressors' – He would be counted among rebels. Rebels carry swords or other weapons. Therefore, they had to have swords with them in order for scripture to be fulfilled. Jesus' mission was to fulfill all the Law and the Prophets so His people would recognize Him as their Messiah. Jesus was completing the Old Covenant in order to bring in the New Covenant.

Do you see why Jesus tells us to be careful what we are hearing? If we're not careful, we will all be running around swinging swords and cutting off ears, leaving people deaf and in pain from what we are wielding!

In addition to reading what I've been taught something says instead of reading what it actually says (and I have many more examples), there are also spiritual meanings for words that cannot be interpreted from my natural filters and experiences. Today I often say, "He likes to speak 'mystery' instead of English!" At times this has frustrated me, but over time I have simply realized I was on an adventure to learn the language of Heaven. I was keenly aware when I heard Him speak to me, I had to pause from acting on what I 'heard' and press in deeper to Him for His meaning. During this time, my prayers were often focused on asking Him to download His dictionary into me so I would operate from His definitions and not what I'd learned things meant from this world. This is simply part of renewing the mind to align with the plumb line of Heaven. If we are to rule and reign in that Kingdom, we need to understand its language, economy, and motivations.

I'm still on my journey, and am certain there is much more for me to learn. What I share in these pages are some of the course corrections He's made for my benefit so far. I pray they benefit you as well. The moment we were born from above, we began our training for a different Kingdom. We have our operating manual in His Word, but if we are trapped in the constraints of our language and mindset about (not to mention our emotional responses to) the meanings of the words we are familiar with, we will not fully know and understand what He speaks. One clear directive He gave me early on was, "Never read My Word without putting on heart-shaped glasses." Everything must be filtered through the lens of love, because He is love. You will find 'Love' even required a course correction in my own understanding before my heart-shaped glasses worked properly. I don't know a lot more than I do know. This adventure into His Kingdom is exhilarating, challenging, and full of wonder if you are ready to learn "all things new" (Revelation 21:5).

I encourage you, as you digest each word, to take time to assess what's new for you, what's challenging for you, and what you need to test for yourself as a good Berean (Acts 17:11).

The words in this 'dictionary' are not arranged in alphabetical order. My worldly understanding would have had me present the content to you that way. He directed a different arrangement for our unpacking. I even planned an unconventional book format to help us break out of our programmed notions about how a book should look. My original design was a 2-column, landscape format that would open from bottom to top instead of right to left. I was assured this was possible in advance of finalizing the manuscript. However, at the time of final submission, I learned that the publishing system would not accommodate that format, requiring both the manuscript and cover to be redesigned at the last minute. What an incredible parable of the constraints we have in this world! This example of a small obstacle is precisely how we are pressed to conform and get stuck in a pre-formulated and defined understanding which limits the abundant possibilities available to us in the Kingdom of God. This world doesn't know how to contain 'all things are possible.' The definitions and limitations of understanding we have been immersed in our whole lives all have to get renewed with Kingdom meanings and definitions. I have a hunch that all the books in heaven open from the bottom to the top – or at least it's possible!

It's just like Him to sneak in one last-minute nugget for us! As we position ourselves to learn the language of heaven, let's see what He wants to 'say' in both His order of choice and the words themselves.

LEARNING LANGUAGE

I recently engaged in training to teach English as a Second Language (ESL) to children in China. The most important thing to remember when instructing others in a foreign language is your language is foreign to them. Seems obvious, right? You are taking a familiar 'object' or 'context' they understand in their native language and are introducing a new vocabulary; teaching new words for things they already know the meaning of.

The techniques to engage the students are strategic. You cannot just jump in and start using your words alone to instruct them. They have no idea what you are saying. Total Physical Response (TPR) is a dual language method developed by James Asher. Consider his understanding from observations of young children learning their first language. Asher noticed these interactions between parents and children often took the form of speech from the parent followed by a physical response from the child. Based on his observations, he made three hypotheses:

1. Language is learned primarily by listening.
2. Language learning must engage the right hemisphere of the brain.

3. Learning language should not involve any stress.

TPR is based on the coordination of language and physical movement. Instructors give commands to students in the target language, and students respond with whole-body actions. The listening and responding (with actions) is both a means of quickly recognizing meaning in the language being learned, and a means of passively learning the structure of the language itself.

In addition to connecting language and physical movement, it is important to speak slowly, clearly, and precisely. Physical gestures to demonstrate what you are saying or asking are necessary for communication in the teaching process. For example, if you are teaching the word "apple," you would show a picture of an apple and ask, "What do you see?" The student will not even understand the question you are asking at the outset. To express "What," you would say the word "what" while placing your hands, palms up, near your shoulders and shrugging your shoulders. You might also scratch your head with a quizzical look. To demonstrate your words "do you," you will point to the child so they associate "you" with their self as you say, "you." As you say, "see," you might point to your eyes, form circles with your hands around your eyes, or form a flat palm and place it at your eyebrows to demonstrate that you are looking at something. As you can see, communicating and relaying understanding is a slow and meticulous process.

This exchange would look like this:

Precision in the pronunciation of words and distinct letter sounds is critical. To indicate to the student you want them to focus on what you are "sounding," you would place your index finger on your chin directly below your mouth as you slowly make the sound of the letter or the word. This focuses the child on the movements your mouth and tongue make as you sound out the letter or word.

When it comes to letters, you want to say the letter "name" and then make the letter "sound." For example, you might use a flashcard with both a big and small "Mm" on it. You would place your finger on your chin, under your mouth while you say "'Em." You would repeat the name of the letter at least three times and indicate they are to say the name of the letter by pointing to them, and then placing your hand behind your ear to show you want to hear them say it.

You would point to the capital 'M' and say "big 'Em'" while gesturing 'big' with your hands. You would point to the lower case 'm' and say "small 'Em'" while gesturing 'small' with your hands.

Then you would teach the sound by saying, "The letter 'em' makes the 'mmm' (not 'muh') sound." You would then make the sound of the letter at least three times and repeat the gesture of pointing to them and placing your hand behind your ear to indicate they are to say the sound of the letter.

This exchange would look like this:

Stress-free learning requires there be no fear of failure. All of the interactions must be bathed in high energy, playfulness, cheerfulness with lots of smiles, recognition for both effort and accomplishment, and, of course, rewards. To maintain the child's engagement and focus, you must be engaging, enthusiastic, and encouraging.

Show them 'Good Job' for trying and/or getting it right. If they need to try again, simply say it again, slowly and precisely, and indicate you want to hear them say it again. You do not want to show disappointment or tell them they did it wrong. They are learning. Trying is good and needs to be acknowledged. Simply do it again.

'High Fives' are great recognition for when they get it right. Add any rewards-tracking system to keep them encouraged and engaged.

As you can tell, the process is slow and may feel tedious. Patience and a willingness to look foolish is necessary. You will likely appear a bit silly at times to capture a child's attention and keep them focused on what you are teaching them. You can have no fear of embarrassment. You must meet them at their appropriate level of understanding and age.

When we ourselves have mastered something – anything – we can easily forget what it was like before we knew what we now know. Redefining something we already 'know' with something new which needs to either replace or refine what we think we know fully is more difficult than learning from scratch.

Consider that.

This is God's great undertaking for all His children. He is patient, and the demonstration of His 'language' (His Word) toward us is shockingly foolish (1 Corinthians 1:27). This is where all of us start when we are born into a new Kingdom. If the above approach feels childish, remember this learning is intended for children who have to replace what they currently know with something new, or something more. That's us.

Think about Adam, walking with his Creator, being told he will 'die' if he eats from the Tree of the Knowledge of Good and Evil. What is 'die'? He could not possibly understand what that word even meant. Nothing had ever died. Without experience, it's just a word. Apart from God imparting His meanings and definitions of things to us, our default understandings from this world are associated with our flesh. There is 'flesh and organ die' and then there is 'spirit die.' They are not the same. Adam experienced both because he had experienced both 'life' and 'Life.' Our association with 'die' today is primarily the 'flesh and organ die.'

Think about teaching a small child 'hot' and 'cold'. Saying the words over and over with a variety of inflections in your voice may transmit some indication of the 'goodness' or 'badness' of these words, but until the child feels 'hot' and 'cold' they won't understand. And truthfully, neither one is 'bad.' Both are 'good' for their intended purposes.

The most significant difference between teaching a new language of words to someone, such as ESL, and teaching Heaven as a Second Language (HSL) is not about learning a new word for the red, juicy piece of fruit in your hand which you call 'apple,' but about learning a new definition for a word you think you already understand. This new definition includes the full meaning and accurate intention, so we can have correct emotional responses connected to it.

It would be like learning an 'apple' is not a red, juicy piece of fruit, but something you've never seen, touched, or tasted before.

So, where ESL teaches new vocabulary to a known context, with HSL, God is teaching new context into our known vocabulary. The result is we live in this world with dual definitions of the language we know: one that applies to the kingdom of the world and one that applies to the Kingdom of God.

The world has imparted meanings and definitions of things which work here, in this world. The Kingdom of Heaven is altogether different. Things don't operate there the same way they do here. The words we are familiar with don't mean the same thing in the context of the eternal Kingdom of the Spirit of Love, Light, Grace and Truth. We have to learn a new way entirely.

Isaiah 55:8-9 (NASB):

"For My thoughts are not your thoughts,
Nor are your ways My ways," declares the LORD.
"For as the heavens are higher than the earth,
So are My ways higher than your ways
And My thoughts than your thoughts.

Are you ready?

CORRECTION

We think in pictures, smells, sounds, and textures. The words we read or hear engage our mind with all of our senses. So, what do you see when you read the word 'correction?' Do you see red marks or 'X's'? Do you see an 'F'? Do you see a finger pointing or wagging? Do you see the metal bars of an institution? What do you hear? Do you hear a sharp, loud voice? Do you hear words of shame? Do you hear laughter? Do you feel your nose pressed into a corner, or your ear being tugged on?

I begin with this word because we are embarking on learning new things, and we have all sorts of emotional responses, impressions, and images from our experiences of being 'corrected' in this world, many of which can hinder the process of learning anything new. We need to 'correct' our understanding of 'correction' first!

Our creator designed us with an amazing capacity to learn, unlearn, and relearn. Without this capability it would be impossible for us to grow in understanding, even to repent and renew our minds about our very existence and our relation to eternity.

The systems which have been constructed in this world have taught us correction is about adhering to certain standards and measures. Whether we are demonstrating the ability to regurgitate information which we may or may not have actually learned, to test well, to behave according to prescriptive models, to meet regulated expectations, or to advance toward a scripted success which may not allow the fullest expression of our being, we submit to the program based on our carrot-stick training. Do you see any of those elements in your own life?

When the Kingdom of Heaven becomes the basis for your life, a collision with the training you've received from this world occurs. There must be. After all, if heaven operated on the same premise as the world does, heaven would not be any different. The greatest challenge we face in learning and applying the truth of the Kingdom is to realize it functions counterintuitively – inside-out and upside-down – from the reality of our daily existence here. We will ever be confronted with applying a different reality as we exist in this place which is now a 'foreign' abode for us.

Here's a great Biblical example of the type of inverted thinking and perception we must have. In Acts 5, the apostles are brought before the Sanhedrin Council and admonished to stop talking about Jesus. As part of that ruling, the apostles are flogged as punishment, and a deterrent from furthering the gospel message.

> Acts 5:41 (NASB): *So they [the apostles] went on their way from the presence of the Council, rejoicing that they had been considered worthy to suffer shame for His name.*

Correction is necessary. Not a carrot-stick, punishment, behavior modification type of correction. Its purpose is specific. We must unlearn and relearn. We have to unlearn the ways we have been previously trained to operate effectively and efficiently to establish ourselves here. We must now learn how to be established in the ways of a different Kingdom. This correction is evidence, worthy of incredible rejoicing, for we have been chosen to exist for eternity in an altogether different realm where we will rule and reign. If we are to rule and reign in this entirely different Kingdom, it is imperative we understand its government and economy.

Correction is great news! The emotional response we've acquired in the negative application of correction we've received here must be converted to joy in correction from a Father who is preparing us. It's proof of our chosenness to rule and reign. We should in the least cooperate, and in the greatest pursue it with great enthusiasm! The pain of our discomfort is evidence of change.

Hebrews 12:4-17 (NASB): *[A Father's Discipline]*
You have not yet resisted to the point of

shedding blood in your striving against sin; and you have forgotten the exhortation which is addressed to you as sons,

"MY SON, DO NOT REGARD LIGHTLY THE DISCIPLINE OF THE LORD,
NOR FAINT WHEN YOU ARE REPROVED BY HIM;
FOR THOSE WHOM THE LORD LOVES HE DISCIPLINES,
AND HE SCOURGES EVERY SON WHOM HE RECEIVES."

It is for discipline that you endure; God deals with you as with sons; for what son is there whom his father does not discipline? But if you are without discipline, of which all have become partakers, then you are illegitimate children and not sons. Furthermore, we had earthly fathers to discipline us, and we respected them; shall we not much rather be subject to the Father of spirits, and live? For they disciplined us for a short time as seemed best to them, but He disciplines us for our good, so that we may share His holiness. All discipline for the moment seems not to be joyful, but sorrowful; yet to those who have been trained by it, afterwards it yields the peaceful fruit of righteousness.

Therefore, strengthen the hands that are weak and the knees that are feeble, and make straight paths for your feet, so that the limb which is lame may not be put out of joint, but rather be healed.

Pursue peace with all men, and the sanctification without which no one will see the Lord. See to it that no one comes short of the grace of God; that no root of bitterness springing up causes trouble, and by it many be defiled; that there be no immoral or godless person like Esau, who sold his own birthright for a single meal. For you know that even afterwards, when he desired to inherit the blessing, he was rejected, for he found no place for repentance, though he sought for it with tears.

So what does correction in the Kingdom of God look like? As the first word in this language lesson, how does this new definition, understanding the full meaning and accurate intention for correction, change your emotional responses?

OUR FATHER,
who art in heaven

Looking for PROOF...

Let's gladly and gratefully receive life-giving correction for our eternal destiny!

A good place to start is by getting to know the One who is training us.

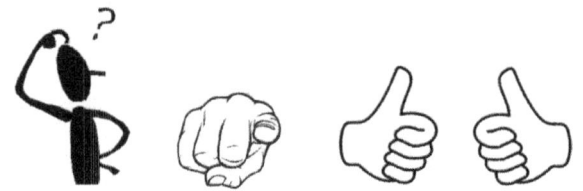

FATHER

Understanding 'Father' is mission-critical. Who is this One correcting us? What are His motivations? Are we interested in ruling and reigning under His government anyway? What kind of 'Father' is He?

What do you see or feel when you read the word 'father?' What have your experiences of the natural father chosen for you in this world taught you? Is 'father' absent, distant, harsh, self-serving, angry, abusive, inappropriate, addicted, regimented, dismissive, belittling, doting, protective, extravagant, engaged, gentle, indulging, instructive, or interested? Is your 'inner' child fearful, shamed, insecure, ignored, invisible, cowering, aggressive, rebellious, silent, strong, stable, or confident? Who do you allow into the role of 'father?' What qualifies them?

Let's consider that the best of earthly fathers fall short of the glory of God. This must be true, as we all have (Romans 3:23). None of them are perfect, nor parent perfectly. Evidently, any impression of 'father' which we've acquired from our experiences with any human 'father' pales to varying degrees in comparison with the Father of Heaven. In fact, Jesus commands us 'adopted' children to call no one on earth 'father.'

> Matthew 23:9 (NASB): *Do not call anyone on earth your father; for One is your Father, He who is in heaven.*

If we acknowledge the truth this Father from above only adopts His children, apart from His only begotten Son, Jesus, then we must conclude that He knew there would be a need for adoption. We need the One Father, who is in Heaven.

> Ephesians 1:3-6 (NASB): *Blessed be the God and Father of our Lord Jesus Christ, who has blessed us with every spiritual blessing in the heavenly places in Christ, just as He chose us in Him before the foundation of the world, that we would be holy and blameless before Him. In love He predestined us to adoption as sons through Jesus Christ to Himself, according to the kind*

intention of His will, to the praise of the glory of His grace, which He freely bestowed on us in the Beloved.

Romans 8:14-17 (NASB): *For all who are being led by the Spirit of God, these are sons of God. For you have not received a spirit of slavery leading to fear again, but you have received a spirit of adoption as sons by which we cry out, "Abba! Father!" The Spirit Himself testifies with our spirit that we are children of God, and if children, heirs also, heirs of God and fellow heirs with Christ, if indeed we suffer with Him so that we may also be glorified with Him.*

What child needs to be adopted? A child who has been abandoned, alienated, or separated from relationship in even the slightest extreme. Think about that. Whether your experience was negative or the best you could have imagined, it fell short of God's glory and intention. Either way, things were out of heavenly order. It can be just as difficult to trust a gentle lovingkindness you never experienced as it is to receive severe correction if a doting and adoring earthly father never brought needed adjustments. We can rejoice at the inadequacy of our natural father's capabilities, and our own, if we ourselves are parents. This inability to reach the glory of the 'Father' who yearns with jealousy to 'Father' us in perfection, prepares us and qualifies each of us for an unrevokable adoption which settles our belonging and eternal inheritance.

Let's be honest though, being adopted by a different father from the one we have experienced means we have to get to know a new father. His attributes, motivations, and ways of dealing with us are not the same. Our experiences have provided filters through which we read, interpret and understand His interactions with us. The template in our mind must be corrected with His own interpretation of Himself for us to grow in our relationship with Him. Our response to His correction must be a willingness to draw near, to get close to Him (James 4:8).

He is not stand-offish, but rather waiting patiently for us to be ready to be close. In fact, 'Abba' is an up-close term. The sense is 'Daddy' or 'Papa' as opposed to the often formal rendering of 'Father.' He won't impose Himself, insist, force, or push a relationship on us we are not open to for a multitude of reasons. He does this out of love which recognizes our 'father' experience may have left us wounded and scarred, or blinded to and undesirous of needed training. He is very patient and gentle in pursuing us, until we desire to draw near. He also will not change who He is to accommodate our preferences for a 'father.' He IS. His holiness stamps His character just as firmly as His love defines His nature. We must acknowledge our inadequacy, need, and depravity for there ever to be a truthful and authentic relationship. He solves it all when we do.

> Exodus 34:5-7 (NASB): *The LORD descended in the cloud and stood there with [Moses] as he called upon the name of the LORD. Then the LORD passed by in front of him and proclaimed, "The LORD, the LORD God, compassionate and gracious, slow to anger, and abounding in lovingkindness and truth; who keeps lovingkindness for thousands, who forgives iniquity, transgression and sin; yet He will by no means leave the guilty unpunished, visiting the iniquity of fathers on the children and on the*

grandchildren to the third and fourth generations."

Romans 11:22 (NASB): *Behold then the kindness and severity of God; to those who fell, severity, but to you, God's kindness, if you continue in His kindness; otherwise you also will be cut off.*

So what does Our Heavenly Father really look like? How does this new definition, understanding the full meaning and accurate intention of His role and activity in our lives, change your emotional responses in His interactions with you?

'Father' is declared to 'be love.' (1 John 4:8) We have learned many definitions and expressions of love in this world. We must know His before we can fully receive it and rightly interpret the motivations of His activity based on His own disclosure of Himself and His love. This would be a great place to go next.

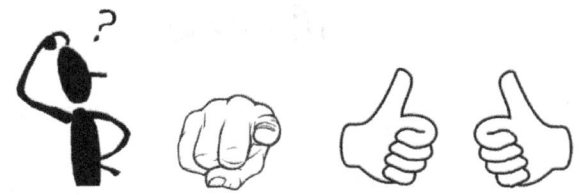

LOVE

We 'love' a lot, don't we? We use this expression in a broad context in our current culture. In ancient languages, various words differentiated between heartfelt attachment, familial affections, physical chemistry, and the deepest levels of commitment. We have one word, so we use it for everything from people to pets to purses to popcorn.

Regardless of the object, we typically associate love as an emotion of attachment which feels good and is pleasurable. For most, as it relates to personal relationships, love is a shared, reciprocal flow of affection and enjoyment.

What do you love? Who do you love? When you read the word 'love,' what is the first attachment that comes to mind? Is it parents, a spouse, a best friend, children or grandchildren? Or is it a passion you have for a certain activity or something you aspire to do? Maybe it's a favorite memory or place. Regardless of where your heart is drawn most powerfully, you feel the emotion just from thinking about it, don't you? Have you ever experienced the pain of unreciprocated love or affection?

This world offers us a lot of things to love. We're acclimated to having vast possibilities for enjoyment and pleasure. Is it possible the dilution of the meaning and its truest expression and experience directly correlates to the plethora of readily available options which allure us into shallow, self-focused pleasures and experiences?

Matthew 24:12 (NASB): *Because lawlessness is increased, most people's love will grow cold.*

Apart from getting clear about the character and nature of Our Father in Heaven, understanding the love of the Kingdom is probably the most paramount undertaking. In fact, to truly know Our Father, we must grasp the love which flows in His Kingdom. Clearly, this love is different from the love we experience in this world. In fact, we are told once we truly grasp the love of the Father, we won't love this world or anything in it any longer.

1 John 2:15 (NASB): *[Do Not Love the World] Do not love the world nor the things in the world. If anyone loves the world, the love of the Father is not in him.*

Jesus is really clear about our natural propensity to love those who love us back, those who are most like us, those who do nice things for us, those who live up to our expectations or standards. We receive no eternal reward for that because there's nothing special about it. It's basic animal nature.

> Matthew 5:46 (NASB): *For if you love those who love you, what reward do you have? Do not even the tax collectors do the same?*

> Luke 6:35 (NASB): *But love your enemies, and do good, and lend, expecting nothing in return; and your reward will be great, and you will be sons of the Most High; for He Himself is kind to ungrateful and evil men.*

Love loves because it is love and can do no differently. If it were dependent on anything external to determine its ability to love, it would relinquish its power to that external element.

We cannot have a full discussion about the love of God without considering His wrath. Think about that for a moment. If it is true, and it is, that God IS Love, then that means every expression of Himself is, in some way, a demonstration of love. How can His wrath fit within the framework of love? Is it possible we have inaccurately defined His wrath and this causes us to misunderstand His love?

What do you imagine when you read the word 'wrath?' Do you hear 'punishment' and 'hate?' How can God hate with such a vengeance and 'be love' at the same time? What kind of god destroys people who make mistakes and aren't perfect? What kind of 'walking on eggshells' existence has this God of 'wrath' created for people? Is He a maniacal ego-driven narcissist? How can 'love' conceive of hell and eternal torment? What kind of 'children' belong to Him? How can you respond in love to a God of 'wrath?' These are fair questions which deserve answers. God's wrath can never be isolated or separated from His love.

Our first problem with understanding all of these words we are looking at is we do so from our own human nature. Yet God's wrath is not the same as human wrath. It is directed toward a different object and for a different objective than ours.

> James 1:20 (NASB): *...for the anger of man does not achieve the righteousness of God.*

Let's start with how our understanding confuses us. Here's an analogy of how the transition from the Old Covenant to the New Covenant can trip us up. Think about how we instruct young people about sex being wrong and sinful outside of marriage. We rarely explain the psychoemotional reasons, and the emotional memories it creates which will cause obstacles later in life when they determine to make a commitment in marriage. We simply hammer all sorts of negativity into them around sex. Now, when they get married, we tell them to enjoy themselves. What?! Their minds have to adjust to this new perspective, and all the negative hammering can have just as devastating an impact on their marriage as the extra pre-marital experiences and associated memories will. The instruction should be less about 'sin' and more about protecting their future commitment from anything which will taint the full freedom of both people to be authentically themselves without fear of being compared to a previous experience. The understanding of the reason provides the context of love. When we read the Old Covenant apart from the 'why' of God, all we read is He's hammering us.

I remember when God told me to only read His Word with heart-shaped glasses on. The specific book He instructed me to read over and over based on this instruction was Revelation. Each time I would read it, He would tell me to 'come up higher.' I began to rise above my own very limited earth-bound view and understanding of the words and could see how this was playing out from God's view in heaven down through all the heavens to earth. Spiritual and natural things were continuing – unseen and seen.

Let's consider the possibility God's 'wrath' is not against people, but against the disobedient angels which have captivated people and caused them to attach their hearts and identities to things which cause them to be less than who God created them to be. In fact, God's wrath and anger is against those unseen influencers in the spiritual realm, and we are instructed to keep our focus on those unseen influencers as well -- never people. Why would we think if we are instructed by the Holy Spirit to remember *our* fight isn't against people, G*od's* would be?

> Ephesians 6:12 (NASB): *For our struggle is not against flesh and blood, but against the rulers, against the powers, against the world forces of this darkness, against the spiritual forces of wickedness in the heavenly places.*

If we've attached our identity to what they're peddling, we will experience God's wrath as if it is against us, when in reality He is coming against that god and trying to destroy it to free us so we will see how it has imprisoned us from the greatness God authored for our lives.

I'm not an expert on hell as a real place because I've never been there, though I've tasted it here. There are obviously many things I do not know, but we are all to be studiers of the scriptures ourselves, so I've studied. And I continue to study. I do know there are four different words translated "hell" in the Bible and have researched the subject extensively over the years. I'm not going to expound on it here, but encourage you to search this out. A good place to start is "The Origin and History of the Doctrine of Endless Punishment" by Thomas B. Thayer. Here, I want us to understand the paradox of 'wrath' being an expression of God's love more than defining the locale of any 'hell.'

The Bible tells us God created a place for, or condition of, imprisonment of these fallen angels who have disobeyed God's design and purpose for them, and are leading His prized creation astray (2 Peter 2:4, Jude 6-8). God's armies are warring throughout the heavens all the way down to earth to destroy anything which traps us in the snares. God sent His Son as a demonstration of His true nature and the lengths He will go to show us how much He longs for us to let go of every false god devised by these disobedient angels as a trusted source. Because He is love, He must not allow these other 'gods' to rule and reign over our hearts and minds; these 'gods' who destroy His intent for *us* to rule and reign. We are the object of His love and He has a plan for each of us in His Kingdom. His wrath-filled, jealous, passionate love for us is coming against everything that is carrying us away from Him. We get to participate in His advancement of love, grace, hope and truth if we choose. If we will not let go of these false sources that have formed us into what we were never intended to be, we will perish. God's desire is not one single person perish – for all to let go of the identities they have been allured into believing they are, instead of who He created them to be. The wrong identities and the associated behaviors won't work in heaven. They must be separated out.

Revelation 20:1-4a, 7-10 (NASB): *Then I saw an angel coming down from heaven, holding the key of the abyss and a great chain in his hand. And he laid hold of the dragon, the serpent of old, who is the devil and Satan, and bound him for a thousand years; and he threw him into the abyss, and shut it and sealed it over him, so that he would not deceive the nations any longer, until the thousand years were completed; after these things he must be released for a short time.*

Then I saw thrones, and they [people who let go of the false sources and identities] *sat on them, and judgment was given to them. ...*

When the thousand years are completed, Satan will be released from his prison, and will come out to deceive the nations which are in the four corners of the earth, Gog and Magog, to gather them together for the war; the number of them is like the sand of the seashore. And they came up on the broad plain of the earth and surrounded the camp of the saints and the beloved city, and fire came down from heaven and devoured them. And the devil who deceived them was thrown into the lake of fire and brimstone, where the beast and the false prophet are also; and they will be tormented day and night forever and ever.

As I sat for months reading and re-reading Revelation and studying with my heart-shaped glasses, I noticed for the first time there are only two places in scripture which mention forever and ever, day and night torment. In the passage above torment is reserved for the devil, beast, and false prophet. Right afterward comes the white throne judgment of people, which we will look at in a minute. First, let's look at the other 'forever and ever torment' – for those who worship the beast.

Revelation 14:9-11 (NASB): *Then another angel, a third one, followed them, saying with a loud voice, "If anyone worships the beast and his image, and receives a mark on his forehead or on his hand, he also will drink of the wine of the wrath of God, which is mixed in full strength in the cup of His anger; and he will be tormented with fire and brimstone in the presence of the holy angels and in the presence of the Lamb. And the smoke of their torment goes up forever and ever; they have no rest day and night, those who worship the beast and his image, and whoever receives the mark of his name."*

A couple of differentiations I noticed between the Revelation 14:11 and 20:10 forever and ever torment in the original language is that the best interpretation for 'torment' in 14:11 is "examination by torture" while that in 20:10 is "to afflict, torment; to be afflicted, tormented, pained, by diseases; to be tossed, agitated, as by the waves." So the pronouncement for worshipers of the beast is for the purpose of examination, whereas for the devil, beast, and false prophet is simply for torment.

A difference between 'forever and ever' also exists. In 14:11 the original words are "eis aiõn aiõn" where 'aiõn' means an era or age as it relates to the material universe, the present order of nature, and the natural condition of man. I wonder if this literally means for two eras or ages. I honestly don't know, but that is what it looked like to me. In 20:10 the original words are "eis ho aiõn ho ho" which is best rendered "for all time (ages)." This devil, beast, and false prophet 'forever and ever' is the same as the 'forever and ever' of His honor, His glory, His reign, His throne, His dominion, His life, our reign, and the rising smoke of the great harlot's burning (reference Ephesians 3:21; Philippians 4:20; 1 Timothy 1:17; 2 Timothy 4:18; Hebrews 1:8; Hebrews 13:21; 1 Peter 4:11, 5:11; Revelation 1:6, 4:9-10, 5:13, 7:12, 10:6, 11:15, 15:7, 19:3, 22:5).

Revelation 14:11 for worshipers of the beast is a different 'forever and ever' which appears to be two ages long intended for examination, not eternal torment.

Now let's return to the white throne judgment which immediately follows the devil, beast, and false prophet being thrown into the lake of brimstone (or sulfur) and fire for the 'forever and ever' of God's existence.

Revelation 20:11-15 (NASB): *Then I saw a great white throne and Him who sat upon it, from whose presence earth and heaven fled away, and no place was found for them. And I saw the dead, the great and the small, standing before the throne, and books were opened; and another book was opened, which is the book of life; and the dead were judged from the things which were written in the books, according to their deeds. And the sea gave up the dead which were in it, and death and Hades gave up the dead which were in them; and they were judged, every one of them according to their deeds. Then death and Hades were thrown into the lake of fire. This is the second death, the lake of fire. And if anyone's name was not found written in the book of life, he was thrown into the lake of fire.*

Though I'm not expounding on hell here, I do think it's important to notice, Hades (translated 'hell' in many Bible translations) is destroyed, so therefore it cannot be eternal.

Now, let's consider the distinctions between 'fire and brimstone' and simply 'fire.' The only other place in scripture where we see fire and brimstone is in the destruction of Sodom (Genesis 19). Fire and sulfur is connected to destruction, where fire is for refining and purification (Zechariah 13:9; Malachi 3:2; Matthew 3:11). In the original language, the lake of fire mentioned in Revelation 20:14 and 15 above does not have 'brimstone.' It does show up again at the conclusion of all things:

Revelation 21:8 (NASB): *But for the cowardly and unbelieving and abominable and murderers and immoral persons and sorcerers and idolaters and all liars, their part will be in the lake that burns with fire and brimstone, which is the second death.*

So this love of God has put in place a rescue mission to recover every created object of His affection. He blocked our way from eating from the Tree of Life so we would not live in an eternal state of 'misidentity,' until He concludes His plan to bring complete judgment and order to anything which chooses not to fulfill the purpose for which He created it. He will also restore us eternally to our intended state (Genesis 3:22-24) – His pre-ordained, pre-scribed (written in Heaven's scrolls) destiny (pre-destination). He has purposed His wrath against every deception and trap which has been set to convince us we are something other than who He created us to be.

He wants us to know His holy character, as well as His loving nature. He exhibits both to us because we don't know Him. His holiness is an expression of His love which desires the highest, most benevolent actions toward and among all His children. He demonstrates He is not distant by entering our full human experience that He may empathize with our blind and unknowing condition, and provide the blood sacrifice which intercedes for us forever. Intercession requires empathy, and empathy requires stepping into the experience of another.

All of this was done (brought about) for you and me. Only those who will not let go of the 'misidentity' and receive the truth of who they truly were created to be will perish in the second death. Only the original purpose of a created thing has a place of fulfillment in the Kingdom of Heaven. If the created thing refuses to fulfill its purpose, it will not exist. Revelation 21:8 does not say anything about forever and ever, day and night torment. Where in the human heart did this imagination originate I wonder. And how often do we read what we've been taught instead of studying the words in front of us? We have eternal life or we don't (1 John 5:12). Death is eternal, an eternal punishment if you will, for anyone who does not have the Son (Matthew 25:46). An eternal legacy of humiliation and disgrace is also punishment. The reputation of our character lives beyond our life.

> Romans 6:23 (NASB): *For the wages of sin is death, but the free gift of God is eternal life in Christ Jesus our Lord.*

What does it say the wages of sin is? Death. What does it *not say* that you have heard added by many teachings? When and how were those additions made? That's worth studying.

> John 3:16 (NASB): *For God so loved the world, that He gave His only begotten Son, that*

whoever believes in Him shall not perish, but have eternal life.

The Greek word for "perish" is "apollymi" and means "to destroy utterly; to kill, to bring to nought, make void; to lose, be deprived of; to be destroyed; to be put to death, to die; to be lost."

Don't miss the contrast is between perishing (deprived of life) and eternal life. This contrast shows up in numerous places in the New Testament, and Jesus' own words reflect the distinction between "perishing" and "eternal life." He clearly states in Matthew 10:28 that man can kill the body, but God can "apollymi" both the body and soul.

Love in the Kingdom is expressed by each unique created object fulfilling the Father's intended purpose. Fulfilling His purpose is its 'life.' Submitted obedience to His purpose expresses love because this demonstrates an understanding that His intention for all He creates is rooted in perfect benevolence. Submitted obedience desires His perfect benevolence to be fulfilled. Consider the sun, moon, and stars.

1 Corinthians 15:41 (NASB): *There is one glory of the sun, and another glory of the moon, and another glory of the stars; for star differs from star in glory.*

Genesis 1:14-18 (NASB): *Then God said, "Let there be lights in the expanse of the heavens to separate the day from the night, and let them be for signs and for seasons and for days and years; and let them be for lights in the expanse of the heavens to give light on the earth"; and it was so. God made the two great lights, the greater light to govern the day, and the lesser light to govern the night; He made the stars also. God placed them in the expanse of the heavens to give light on the earth, and to govern the day and the night, and to separate the light from the darkness; and God saw that it was good.*

The sun is greater in terms of its light production, not in terms of importance. The moon doesn't compete with the sun for significance, but without waver follows its course and satisfies the Father's purpose in His creation of it. The sun, moon, and stars all play their role in providing light, signs, and announcements of appointed seasons on God's calendar in service to us. They were created to provide warmth, life, light, and to communicate to us. They are signals which point to God's appointed times or scheduled visitations. They are dutiful to that purpose, which serves us, not themselves.

Ok, so those are elements of creation which weren't designed with a free will. They don't argue with their creator about their form or function. Aren't you grateful? Can you imagine if the moon had a hankering to compete with the sun and rebelled against its assignment?

Consider Jesus.

Hebrews 10:5-7 (NASB): *Therefore, when He comes into the world, He says,*

"SACRIFICE AND OFFERING YOU HAVE NOT DESIRED,
BUT A BODY YOU HAVE PREPARED FOR ME;
IN WHOLE BURNT OFFERINGS AND sacrifices FOR SIN YOU
HAVE TAKEN NO PLEASURE.
"THEN I SAID, 'BEHOLD, I HAVE COME

(IN THE SCROLL OF THE BOOK IT IS WRITTEN OF ME)
TO DO YOUR WILL, O GOD.'"

John 10:17 (NASB): *For this reason the Father loves Me, because I lay down My life so that I may take it again.*

Matthew 26:42 (NASB): *He went away again a second time and prayed, saying, "My Father, if this cannot pass away unless I drink it, Your will be done."*

Jesus came with a specific purpose from the Father. His obedience was perfected by fully accomplishing that purpose, so we could be reconciled (Hebrews 5:8). And it brought Him joy to do it (Hebrews 12:2). So what does Kingdom-love look like? How does this new definition, understanding the full meaning and accurate intention of all God's expressions of love, change your emotional responses to His choices for expressing love to you?

Think about how Jesus taught His disciples to pray in Matthew 6:10 (NASB):

> 'Your kingdom come.
> Your will be done,
> On earth as it is in heaven.

Reconsider the sun, moon, and stars. The Father's will is accomplished in the heavens because each object stays within its design and purpose. In that same way, Jesus fulfilled His Father's will for Him here on earth. He was obedient to the purpose for which the body had been prepared for him. It was not in service to himself, but in service to the Father's plan for reuniting us with our eternal destiny of abiding in an unfathomable love. This is the love we must learn. We must love our unique design, the purpose for which we were designed, the service we were designed to accomplish, and the One Who designed us and prepared the service to perfectly suit His plans. The world's loves will not operate in heaven. They are too low, too shallow, too short, and too narrow.

1 John 2:4-6 (NASB): *The one who says, "I have come to know Him," and does not keep His commandments, is a liar, and the truth is not in him; but whoever keeps His word, in him the love of God has truly been perfected. By this we know that we are in Him: the one who says he abides in Him ought himself to walk in the same manner as He walked.*

1 John 4:18 (NASB): *There is no fear in love; but perfect love casts out fear, because fear involves punishment, and the one who fears is not perfected in love.*

The apostle Paul gives a robust definition of Kingdom love. This love flows from its originating Source – Our Father.

1 Corinthians 13:1-7 (NASB): *[The Excellence of Love] If I speak with the tongues of men and of angels, but do not have love, I have become a noisy gong or a clanging cymbal. If I have the gift of prophecy, and know all mysteries and all knowledge; and if I have all faith, so as to remove mountains, but do not have love, I am nothing. And if I give all my possessions to feed the poor, and if I surrender my body to be burned, but do not have love, it profits me nothing.*

Love is patient, love is kind and is not jealous; love does not brag and is not arrogant, does not act unbecomingly; it does not seek its own, is not provoked, does not take into account a wrong suffered, does not rejoice in unrighteousness, but rejoices with the truth; bears all things, believes all things, hopes all things, endures all things.

The Father loves because it is His nature. His love is not dependent on us. It simply IS. It's incredible His love doesn't "seek its own" – doesn't demand its own way. It makes a way at its own cost.

That's definitely a love not of this world. Love is the very atmosphere of heaven. We must be trained in it here in order to exist eternally there. Let's give our attention next to this realm.

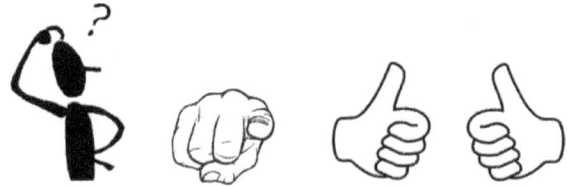

Heaven

What is heaven? Where is heaven? What do you think of when you read the word 'heaven?' Do you see everyone floating on clouds? Do you see pearly gates with a gatekeeper checking the 'naughty' and 'nice' list like Santa Claus? What are people doing there? Is it an eternal praise and worship service? Do your imaginations leave you bored?

Our questions about heaven reveal our attachments to this world – the things and experiences we have here. I can understand and appreciate that. Our hearts have connected to things here. We want to know about our pets, our loved ones, our favorite activities and the tangible things which give us pleasure here.

"...Wish I'd brought a magazine."

"I miss stress."

GOD, THIS IS BORING

"So you're little Bobbie; well, Rex here has been going on and on about you for the last 50 years."

Heaven is tricky. I have never lived there. Have you? Jesus clearly states He is the only one who can teach us the things of heaven because He alone has come from there to earth.

John 6:38 (NASB): *For I have come down from heaven, not to do My own will, but the will of Him who sent Me.*

John 3:12-13 (NASB): *If I told you earthly things and you do not believe, how will you believe if I tell you heavenly things? No one has ascended into heaven, but He who descended from heaven: the Son of Man.*

What is available for us to know from the Bible? Well, let's start with the understanding 'Heavens' is always plural in Hebrew. In scripture seven different words are translated 'heavens' and, in Hebrew thought, they denote seven different levels. Let's consider each one. (Reference: The One New Man Bible – Glossary)

Isaiah 40:22 talks about God stretching out the heavens like a curtain, spreading them out like a tent to dwell in. That word 'curtain' used to describe the 'heavens' is 'Dok.' Dok is the entire universe, way beyond what we can observe with even the strongest telescope. Dok fades away every morning and returns its display in the evening. It exhibits the daily renewal of creation.

Genesis 1:17 tells us that God set the stars, sun, moon, and planets in the firmament of the heavens. The word for 'firmament' is 'Rakia.' We can see Rakia with the naked eye. It is outer space through which constellations, solar systems, and galaxies maintain their orbits and relationships to one another.

Psalm 78:23-24 tell us of the skies above where the doors of heaven are opened and from which God commanded manna and heavenly grain to be rained down. The word for 'skies' is 'Sheckakim.' This is the atmosphere permeated with His Word, where millstones grind manna for the righteous.

1 Kings 8:13 explains that God has surely built a house of 'habitation' or a place for us to dwell forever. The word for 'habitation' is 'Zevul.' In this location we will find the celestial Jerusalem, Temple, and the altar where Michael offers a sacrifice. Isaiah 63:15a says,

> *Look down from heaven and see from Your holy and glorious habitation (Zevul);...*

Psalm 42:9 describes the place where His ministering angels stay, singing in the night. According to the Psalm, from this place the Lord commands His loving kindness during the day and His song to be with us in the night. The word 'Maon' is used for this 'habitation' as used in Deuteronomy 26:15a:

> Look down from Your holy habitation (Maon), from heaven,...

Deuteronomy 28:12 reveals the place of the Lord's good treasure – the storehouses of snow, rain, hail, whirlwinds, storms, etc. We know this is located in a place in heaven called 'Machon' from 1 Kings 8:39a:

> ...then hear in heaven Your dwelling place (Machon),...

Psalm 104:3 talks about the one who rides on the clouds. The word for 'clouds' is 'Aravot.' This heaven is where righteousness, judgement, and charity are found; the storehouses of life, of peace and blessing, the spirits of righteousness, all with which the Lord will revive the dead. Those we find living here are the Ophannim, Seraphim, holy Chayyot, the ministering angels, the Throne of Glory, and the King of the Universe.

The One New Man Bible Glossary summarizes these seven heavens as follows:

"Notice that the first three represent the universe, the visible night sky and sun, and the atmosphere. These are natural, physical things even when beyond the range of telescope.

Each of the other four levels is both physical and spiritual. Three levels are translated Habitation, but that is not the clue we need. Three levels are populated: Zevul, with the celestial Jerusalem; Maon, with bands of ministering angels; and Aravot, with various heavenly beings, the Throne, and the spirits of the saint. That is probably the level Paul referred to, the third of the populated levels, in 2 Cor. 12:2."

It seems the 'heavens' is a well-ordered, busy place from which the government of the King of King's Kingdom functions.

What else can we learn about the mysteries of the heavens from scripture? We know when Jesus began His ministry, He, like John the Baptist before Him, announced repentance is required because the Kingdom of Heaven is at hand (Matthew 3:2; 4:17). We know when He was baptized by John in the Jordan, the Spirit and voice of God came from the heavens to signify His identity and the Father's pleasure in Him (Matthew 3:16-17).

Jesus tells us who this kingdom, where our Father lives, belongs to, and it apparently has rewards (Matthew 5:3,10,12,16,19,20). He declares that the 'sky' (Sheckakim – see above) will someday pass away (Matthew 5:18; 24:35). Before it passes away, however, He will come on the clouds of the 'sky' (Matthew 26:64). It is a place where we can build a storehouse of treasure for ourselves (Matthew 6:20; 19:21). It holds mysteries which are only made known to those who have been chosen as disciples of Jesus (Matthew 13; 18; 22). It has keys (Matthew 16:19). It is only for those who will become as children (Matthew 18:3-4,10,14; 19:14; Luke 10:21). We will not be married there (Mark 12:25). At the end, these heavens will be shaken (Mark 13:25; Luke 21:26; Hebrews 12:26). He sits there now at the right hand of God (Mark 16:19). Names are recorded in it (Luke 10:20). Everything we have comes from out of heaven (John 3:27). We are currently seated there with Jesus in our spirit (Ephesians 2:4-7). Spiritual forces of wickedness are there which we war against (Ephesians 6:12). Our citizenship is now there (Philippians 3:20). Our hope is laid up there (Colossians 1:5). We have an imperishable inheritance reserved for us there (1 Peter 1:4). They are reserved for fire at the judgment of ungodly men (2 Peter 3:7,10,12). New heavens will come for righteousness alone to dwell (2 Peter 3:13; Revelation 21:1). We will judge the angels (1 Corinthians 6:3).

How does that information shift your imaginations of the heavens? I still don't know the fullness of what eternity in heaven will be or what each of us will be doing, but it sounds far from boring to me. I can imagine endless possibilities. What if, now that God has multiplied His children, He wants to create many universes, all of which will require revelation of His holy character and loving nature? What if we will be emissaries of the King and distributors for the Kingdom to a new creation?

We know there will be no more tears, pain, suffering, or death there (Isaiah 25:8, Revelation 22). There will be nothing to fear (1 John 4:18). We will be incorruptible and have all wisdom (Romans 8:21, Colossians 2:3). We will fully comprehend and see what has been partial and mysterious to this point (1 Corinthians 13:12). Imagine how God can expand with a family in full obedience to His plans. We would all be in the family business – for whatever He determines that business to accomplish! Regardless of what it will be and what we will be doing, God's goodness assures us it will satisfy us deeply, just as it will please Him. We will exist in delight for eternity, feasting on a continuous banquet of Divine fruit.

So, based on the wealth of information we are provided from scripture, do you see anything new? Are you able to envision possibilities you didn't before? How does this new understanding change your emotional responses toward your heavenly home?

It would be a good idea to consider 'family' next since we are God's family, currently in the business together, and we will be for eternity.

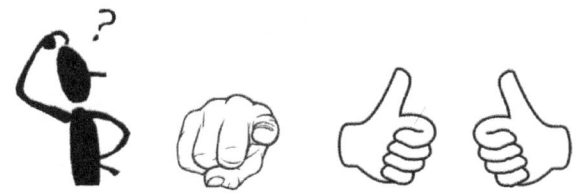

Family

Family forms our roots in this world. Our unique DNA is determined by flesh and blood relationships. When you read the word 'family' what comes to mind? What is your personal family experience? Do you have nostalgic images of the 'perfect' family which you have seen portrayed – a successful father, a mother who may stay at home or have a career of her own, either one or two siblings (based on the 2.5 children average)?

Do you imagine family dinners as the preferred protocol, or a very active, grab-n-go nightly schedule? Do you see game nights, family holidays and vacations, or afternoons of letting yourself in the house and scrounging for dinner on your own? Do you think of daily chores or daily chats about what's going on in your life?

Did you grow up surrounded by grandparents, aunts, uncles, and cousins, or did you grow up disconnected from extended family? Do you have a single-parent home? Are you adopted? Are you raised by extended family members or foster parents, not having either of your parents in your life?

What is 'family' for you, in reality and in your imagination? Have you compared your actual family to an image different from your own? If so, does this cause you to believe you are missing something?

Family is a big deal in our lives. All we absorb, through the umbilical cord in the womb, every initial sound, touch, smell, taste, and sight, as well as the very understanding of our existence in and experience of the world around us is formed and fashioned by these relationships.

Because 'family' in this world is identifiable at a cellular level, not just our household makeup and experiences, we easily buy the 'blood is thicker than water' notion. These attachments run root deep in us. A tough adjustment is required for the Kingdom. Realigning to Jesus' foundation for 'family' can seem incredibly harsh, unless we understand how relationships in the Kingdom work. The truth is the 'spirit' is far more important than blood. Any child who has been adopted will grasp this more easily than those of us who haven't.

Our traditional understanding of 'family' in this world runs through genealogy. It is a linear history which expresses the order through time. Typically, we identify family by biology. As a mother, I have experienced life growing inside of me which then becomes its own being. This allows me to appreciate my mother's experience of me as her child. This chain of flesh and blood reaches through the ages.

Jesus unravels all of this, and it's shocking. Let's listen to his remarks about birth and family relationships from the perspective of our Father above.

> John 3:1-8 (NASB): *[The New Birth] Now there was a man of the Pharisees, named Nicodemus, a ruler of the Jews; this man came to Jesus by night and said to Him, "Rabbi, we know that You have come from God as a teacher; for no one can do these signs that You do unless God is with him." Jesus answered and said to him, "Truly, truly, I say to you, unless one is born again he cannot see the kingdom of God."*
>
> *Nicodemus said to Him, "How can a man be born when he is old? He cannot enter a second time into his mother's womb and be born, can he?" Jesus answered, "Truly, truly, I say to you, unless one is born of water and the Spirit he cannot enter into the kingdom of God. That which is born of the flesh is flesh, and that which is born of the Spirit is spirit. Do not be amazed that I said to you, 'You must be born again.' The wind blows where it wishes and you hear the sound of it, but*

do not know where it comes from and where it is going; so is everyone who is born of the Spirit."

In the Apostle Paul's prayer for the church in Ephesus, he states,

Ephesians 3:14-15 (NASB): *For this reason I bow my knees before the Father, from whom every family in heaven and on earth derives its name,...*

This emphasizes there is only one true Father, the only One Jesus permits the children of the Kingdom to call 'father.' Let's consider Jesus definition of 'family.'

Matthew 12:46-50 (NASB): *[Changed Relationships] While He was still speaking to the crowds, behold, His mother and brothers were standing outside, seeking to speak to Him. Someone said to Him, "Behold, Your mother and Your brothers are standing outside seeking to speak to You." But Jesus answered the one who was telling Him and said, "Who is My mother and who are My brothers?" And stretching out His hand toward His disciples, He said, "Behold My mother and My brothers! For whoever does the will of My Father who is in heaven, he is My brother and sister and mother."*

Luke 14:26 (NASB): *If anyone comes to Me, and does not hate his own father and mother and wife and children and brothers and sisters, yes, and even his own life, he cannot be My disciple.*

This all sounds so harsh, but Jesus is after the realignment of our heart to what defines 'family' in the Kingdom of the Father who birthed us into His family by the Holy Spirit. You see, every single child of the Father entered into the Kingdom at one point and one location in history – the cross, burial, and resurrection of Jesus. Regardless of when you were born in the earthly timeline, from God's perspective your old man died with Jesus on the cross, and your new man was born with Jesus when He stepped out of that tomb alive.

The Kingdom has one Father, and all others are siblings, while in this worldly reality we might have had parents, grandparents, aunts, uncles, cousins, or any other generational relationships. Anyone who does the will of God the Father is a child, and therefore a sibling to all other children throughout all history. If you and your mother are both born again doers of the will of the Father, you are now siblings. If not, you are not related in terms of the Kingdom. If you and your grandfather are both born again doers of the will of the Father, you are now siblings. If not, you are not related in terms of the Kingdom. If you and your child are both born again doers of the will of the Father, you are now siblings. If not, you are not related in terms of the Kingdom. The identifier of relationship is doing the will of the Father, which we cannot know apart from being born again by the Spirit.

You have siblings who were born thousands of years ago, and siblings who live thousands of miles away on the other side of the world. You may not have any Kingdom siblings in the home you are living in, but you have siblings all over the world and throughout history who you have never met. The organizational chart, or 'family tree' in the Kingdom of God is flat – Father and all His children.

This is a huge adjustment to our thinking, which has been rooted in bloodlines, nationalities, and even neighborhoods. Our citizenship is in Heaven, not this world. We are foreigners here. Being a fellow citizen of Heaven, I have siblings all over the globe. Some of them the Lord chose out of China, Africa, Russia, Germany, Vietnam, Hungary, Mexico, Guatemala, England, Indonesia, Iraq, Israel, etc. He chose me out of America, but my citizenship is in Heaven. This citizenship trumps every nationality in this world. My family blankets the earth.

So what does our heavenly family look like? How does this new understanding change your emotional responses to your biological family and your spiritual family here on earth?

And by the Spirit, I know when someone knows my Father or not. There is a family resemblance to our first-born Brother. Because there is only one Holy Spirit, those of this Spirit-birth will walk through this world exhibiting a life which is recognizable and will be marked by the characteristics of our Brother.

Nothing is missing or lacking in the life of this family, regardless of what your experience with or what the structure of your family in this world has been.

Speaking of life, that seems to be a good place to go next.

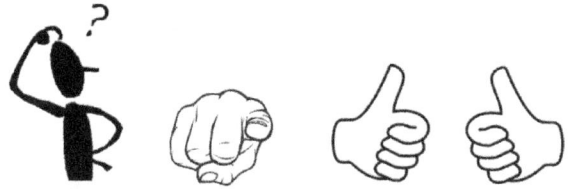

Life

What is 'life?' How do we know something has life? What do you think of when you read the word 'life?' Is it about biology? Can you tell if something has life by activity, movement, or growth? Is it about blood, cells, organs, or DNA? Is it breathing and the flow of oxygen in and out of the lungs? Is it the pumping of blood through the heart? Is it the processing of data all around us through brain function? Is it seeing, hearing, smelling, tasting, or touching? Is it feeling the vast range of emotions? How do you know you have life? When do you know something doesn't have life?

Interestingly, our culture today puts much emphasis on 'work-life balance.' The implication is 'work' and its byproducts are not life or connected to life; that things outside of work are what 'life' is all about. If this is true, we spend a major portion of our life not connected to 'life,' even while our body functions would indicate that we are indeed alive. This means we can be alive and yet not have life. Interesting concept, isn't it?

We also hear 'life' buzzwords in the church today, such as 'blessed' and 'abundant' (John 10:10). What do we mean by those?

What are the distinctions for you?

The first time any word related to 'life' is used in the Bible is in Genesis 1:20, and it refers to 'living creatures.' By this time, God had already created all plants and vegetation, but they are sprouted or produced from the earth and yield or bear after their kind. There is no life-related language in the Biblical understanding of plant growth.

It seems that 'life' is unique to flesh.

> 1 Corinthians 15:39 (NASB): *All flesh is not the same flesh, but there is one flesh of men, and another flesh of beasts, and another flesh of birds, and another of fish.*

> Leviticus 17:11,14 (NASB): *For the life of the flesh is in the blood, and I have given it to you on the altar to make atonement for your souls; for it is the blood by reason of the life that makes atonement.'...*

> *"For as for the life of all flesh, its blood is identified with its life. Therefore I said to the sons of Israel, 'You are not to eat the blood of any*

flesh, for the life of all flesh is its blood; whoever eats it shall be cut off.'

Human life somehow comprehends and knows of eternity; that life is not intended to be extinguished by its antithesis, death. Earlier we mentioned our human work is not a carrier of or connector to life. However, all of God's work is.

Ecclesiastes 3:11 (NASB): *He has made everything appropriate in its time. He has also set eternity in their heart, yet so that man will not find out the work which God has done from the beginning even to the end.*

As disgusting and disturbing as this is, the Satanists' practice of eating the flesh and drinking the blood of human sacrifice is evidence of Satan's belief in the truths of blood-flesh 'life' and eternity. This is the twisted means of achieving eternal life, and the younger the life-source, the more powerful it is believed to be in this demented thinking. The internal truth of eternity combined with the powerful fear of death is all Satan needs to twist and pervert the truth which God discloses. A third truth which he either doesn't comprehend or intentionally does not communicate to those he deceives is eternal life comes only by the Spirit. The solution for the fear of death is understanding the only thing in the flesh is sin and death, but by Spirit-birth we are promised a new and eternal body which is free from both. Once you are Spirit-born and this truth permeates your being, you long for the day when you will be freed from the constraints of your current flesh and blood existence (Romans 7:22-25; 2 Corinthians 5). Death is an affront when we rightly agree with life and its eternal intention, but wrongly attach it to this dust suit. In reality, death becomes freedom.

Hebrews 2:14-16 (NASB): *Therefore, since the children share in flesh and blood, He Himself likewise also partook of the same, that through death He might render powerless him who had the power of death, that is, the devil, and might free those who through fear of death were subject to slavery all their lives. For assuredly He does not give help to angels, but He gives help to the descendant of Abraham.*

1 Corinthians 15:50 (NASB): *[The Mystery of Resurrection] Now I say this, brethren, that flesh and blood cannot inherit the kingdom of God; nor does the perishable inherit the imperishable.*

Satanists who eat human flesh and drink human blood believe they are gaining longer 'life' (because the "life of the flesh is in the blood"), striving for that eternity which is inside, but according to the Bible, they are ingesting greater levels of sin and death, because sin is in the flesh of all born-below humanity.

The book of Romans is probably the most comprehensive New Testament writing about our human 'flesh.'

Romans 7:5,14,18 (NASB): *For while we were in the flesh, the sinful passions, which were aroused by the Law, were at work in the members of our body to bear fruit for death. ... [The Conflict of*

Two Natures] For we know that the Law is spiritual, but I am of flesh, sold into bondage to sin. ...For I know that nothing good dwells in me, that is, in my flesh; for the willing is present in me, but the doing of the good is not.

Romans 8:2-4,6-8 (NASB): *For the law of the Spirit of life in Christ Jesus has set you free from the law of sin and of death. For what the Law could not do, weak as it was through the flesh, God did: sending His own Son in the likeness of sinful flesh and as an offering for sin, He condemned sin in the flesh, so that the requirement of the Law might be fulfilled in us, who do not walk according to the flesh but according to the Spirit. ...*

For the mind set on the flesh is death, but the mind set on the Spirit is life and peace, because the mind set on the flesh is hostile toward God; for it does not subject itself to the law of God, for it is not even able to do so, and those who are in the flesh cannot please God.

Romans 8:11-13 (NASB): *But if the Spirit of Him who raised Jesus from the dead dwells in you, He who raised Christ Jesus from the dead will also give life to your mortal bodies through His Spirit who dwells in you.*

So then, brethren, we are under obligation, not to the flesh, to live according to the flesh— for if you are living according to the flesh, you must die; but if by the Spirit you are putting to death the deeds of the body, you will live.

Let's look at what Jesus discloses about flesh and life in His teachings.

John 3:5-7 (NASB): *Jesus answered, "Truly, truly, I say to you, unless one is born of water and the Spirit he cannot enter into the kingdom of God. That which is born of the flesh is flesh, and that which is born of the Spirit is spirit. Do not be amazed that I said to you, 'You must be born again.'*

John 6:53-57,63 (NASB): *So Jesus said to them, "Truly, truly, I say to you, unless you eat the flesh of the Son of Man and drink His blood, you have no life in yourselves. He who eats My flesh and drinks My blood has eternal life, and I will raise him up on the last day. For My flesh is true food, and My blood is true drink. He who eats My flesh and drinks My blood abides in Me, and I in him. As the living Father sent Me, and I live because of the Father, so he who eats Me, he also will live because of Me. ...*

It is the Spirit who gives life; the flesh profits nothing; the words that I have spoken to you are spirit and are life.

Jesus Christ's blood was pure and His flesh was sinless so He could make this claim, though He is clearly not speaking about eating His actual flesh, but His words, as He states above. Remember, higher thoughts are being communicated by Jesus. The Gospel of John tells us the Word became flesh (John 1:14). I clearly remember when God used this Gospel to communicate to me, "In the beginning was the Word, and the Word was with God, and the Word was God. And I sent my Word in the flesh so that now I can turn your flesh into the Word." This is eternal life.

Satan communicates all his deception at the lowest, natural, literal level. Jesus speaks a higher language. We have to tune in.

In the book of Revelation, Jesus confronts one of the seven churches with their confusion about what it looks like to 'be alive.' They apparently aren't the only ones confused, because they have a reputation of being alive, though Jesus sees beyond outward activity and behaviors. He sees the death inside, just as He could for the whitewashed tombs of the Pharisees (Matthew 23:27).

> Revelation 3:1-2 (NASB): *[Message to Sardis] "To the angel of the church in Sardis write:*
>
> *He who has the seven Spirits of God and the seven stars, says this: 'I know your deeds, that you have a name that you are alive, but you are dead. Walk up, and strengthen the things that remain, which were about to die; for I have not*

found your deeds completed in the sight of My God.

How do you know if you are 'dead' or 'alive?' How does Jesus' life become our very life, leading to eternal life? It comes by losing the 'life' we have formed and fashioned for ourselves; by dying to our definition of 'life' and ingesting the words He communicates to us through active obedience. This is all about carrying your cross. Let's be honest, it's easier to wear a cross than carry one!

Matthew 16:25 (NASB): *For whoever wishes to save his life will lose it; but whoever loses his life for My sake will find it.*

Luke 14:27 (NASB): *Whoever does not carry his own cross and come after Me cannot be My disciple.*

2 Corinthians 4:11 (NASB): *For we who live are constantly being delivered over to death for*

Jesus' sake, so that the life of Jesus also may be manifested in our mortal flesh.

So what does life in the Kingdom of God look like? How does this new definition, understanding the full meaning and accurate expression of life, change your perspective and emotional responses to hardships or challenging circumstances in your life? How does this impact your daily choices?

I find it fascinating that the meaning of the word "persecute" is "to pursue; endeavor earnestly to acquire." Think about that. Persecution in reality is the pursuit of the truest life inside of Christ and a believer. The only way to know if you have 'life' inside of you is to see what comes out of you under pressure and persecution. What if those who persecute are waiting to see what will come out because they want to know if the life you have is real or not? Look at the life that came out of Jesus (Luke 22:47-23:47)!

> 2 Corinthians 5:14-17 (NASB): *For the love of Christ controls us, having concluded this, that one died for all, therefore all died; and He died for all, so that they who live might no longer live for themselves, but for Him who died and rose again on their behalf.*
>
> *Therefore from now on we recognize no one according to the flesh; even though we have known Christ according to the flesh, yet now we know Him in this way no longer. Therefore if anyone is in Christ, he is a new creature; the old*

things passed away; behold, new things have come.

Galatians 5:16-17 (NASB): *But I say, walk by the Spirit, and you will not carry out the desire of the flesh. For the flesh sets its desire against the Spirit, and the Spirit against the flesh; for these are in opposition to one another, so that you may not do the things that you please.*

1 Peter 4:1-2 (NASB): *Therefore, since Christ has suffered in the flesh, arm yourselves also with the same purpose, because he who has suffered in the flesh has ceased from sin, so as to live the rest of the time in the flesh no longer for the lusts of men, but for the will of God.*

Our longing for eternal life has been placed inside of us by God with one clear way to obtain it.

John 1:12-14 (NASB): *But as many as received Him, to them He gave the right to become children of God, even to those who believe in His name, who were born, not of blood nor of the will of the flesh nor of the will of man, but of God.*

John 3:36 (NASB): *He who believes in the Son has eternal life; but he who does not obey the Son will not see life, but the wrath of God abides on him.*

John 5:24 (NASB): *Truly, truly, I say to you, he who hears My word, and believes Him who sent Me, has eternal life, and does not come into judgment, but has passed out of death into life.*

The next best word for us to understand seems to be 'believe.'

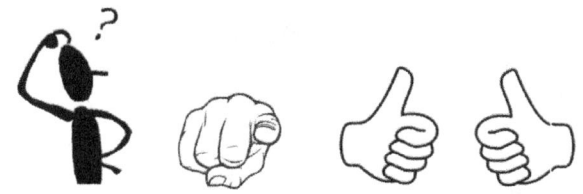

Believe

What does it mean to 'believe' something? Our beliefs are way deep down inside of us; so deep we may not even be aware of them. When you read the word 'believe,' what do you see? Is it a 'like' click or thumbs up for something? Is it giving your agreement or 'yes?' To believe indicates acknowledgement that something is true. How do you know if you really believe something? Is it a good sound bite that rings true, or do you draw from experience?

What we believe shapes our very lives, so it's of great importance to know what we believe. I often say, "You can tell me what you believe, but I'll know what you truly believe by what you do." Simple mental acquiescence is far from the depths required to believe something. It may be the first step, but the finish line is a long way away from basic acknowledgement or agreement.

The clearest way you communicate what you believe is not by telling people what you believe. The thoughts you think between your own two ears, the words you speak in your everyday conversations, and your actions and behaviors are born out of your beliefs. They are fully expressed through every action you take.

As believers of Jesus, we say we believe many things. We have the advantage of seeing the full picture of His earthly life, where those who walked and talked with Him in the flesh had the tangible experience of Him. They lived day-in and day-out with Him and still struggled with believing. Let's look at some examples.

John the Baptist recognized the presence of Jesus from the womb (Luke 1:41,44). He obviously had also received direct revelation from God of Jesus' identity as the Son of God (John 1:19-34). When his personal situation became difficult and unpleasant, he questioned what had been revealed to him.

> Matthew 11:2-3 (NASB): *Now when John, while imprisoned, heard of the works of Christ, he sent word by his disciples and said to Him, "Are You the Expected One, or shall we look for someone else?"*

I find the wording of John's question fascinating. Previously he declared to those around him he had received the direct revelation that the individual whom the dove would rest upon was the Son of God. He agreed because what he had heard and what he saw in that moment matched. Yet, he asks Jesus if He is the "expected one" when his expectations don't match his imprisoned situation.

Though the writings of their prophets clearly foretold hundreds of details about their coming Messiah, the details they paid attention to and the details they missed are revealed by their expectations. All of the details are true, but their focus on the 'cart' which will carry their ultimate deliverance and the firm establishment of God's

Kingdom caused them to miss the 'horse' – the one submitted to the bit placed in His mouth by His Father – the suffering savior who willingly came in weakness to taste death for all humanity. They didn't understand the writings they had studied their whole lives. They had expectations which made it hard to see. They believed in the 'cart' and couldn't accept the 'horse.'

Let's look at another individual, Peter. This exchange between Peter and Jesus is one which, quite honestly, makes me giggle a little because I hear it play out in my head as if it were happening in today's language. Indulge me for a minute and play along as I tell the story as I hear it (Matthew 16:13-23).

Notice my thought bubble as you read. Jesus is really curious about what people are saying about Him and He knows His disciples keep their ear to the ground. They listen to the rumor mill because it's important for them to be recognized as being with someone of importance. They want to know what people are saying because Jesus is making quite a splash out there! And they were specifically chosen by Him; imagine how important that must make them! They have preferential places in this upcoming Kingdom. So, Jesus asks them what they're hearing – "Who do people say that I am?" Well, quite a lot of ideas are floating around. John the Baptist, who had just been beheaded, Elijah, and Jeremiah or another one of their prophets seemed to be the general consensus. All of those seem to indicate some belief in reincarnation to me. But then Jesus asks them directly what *they* think. Peter immediately blurts out, "You are the Christ (Messiah), the Son of the Living God." Now, Jesus knows Peter did not have the knowledge of that truth anywhere inside of him. He knew it was a direct revelation to Peter from His Father, because no one knows the Son except the Father (Matthew 11:27). Jesus affirms what Peter says and acknowledges the source of that information. Because Peter was who the Father chose to receive this revelation, Jesus declares to him the keys of the kingdom will be given to him. Peter will know what has been bound or loosed in heaven so he can bind and loose on earth what agrees with heaven. (We receive this same promise for the keys and access to heaven's activity when the Father chooses us to receive this revelation.)

Shortly after this, Jesus begins telling His disciples what is about to happen; He must go to Jerusalem and suffer a lot of things from the religious leaders, including being killed, but then He would arise from the dead. Now Peter rebukes Jesus for saying these things. Did you get that? Peter rebukes Jesus. And hear the words he uses – "God forbid it, Lord!" In my 'head-story' I can hear Jesus saying something like this, "Umm, I'm the Son of God, remember? My Father told you that. So, if I'm the Son, I think I would know better than you what my Father has said about this, don't you? I have access to what My Father is doing in heaven. You will as well, but you do not, as of yet, apparently. You are concerned with flesh and blood which Satan uses to keep you bound to lower thinking. Don't be a temptation by talking at that level. It gets in the way of my Father's interests which aren't concerned with the dust suit He provided for me to accomplish His plan."

Now my thought bubble fades into the atmosphere. Surely you noticed Peter had direct revelation from the Father of Jesus' identity, yet didn't believe the information Jesus was sharing. Did he really believe the revelation he received?

One more. Let's look at Thomas. I love how Jesus responds to Thomas' lack of belief in His resurrection. And to be honest, they all had the same lack of belief. None of them believed Jesus' instruction of His impending suffering, death, and resurrection after all the times He'd given it or they would have gone to Galilee where He told them He'd meet them (Matthew 26:32). Their vision was focused on the cart. None of them believed His words until they saw Him in front of them – alive. They were mystified, terrified, and confused. Thomas simply didn't believe *them*. He wanted to see for himself, something they had already been afforded. Jesus met his requirement, just as He had known they all needed to see Him before believing. He knew their minds were rooted in a belief about the Messiah which was partial and were unable to comprehend the missing pieces they had read of but never seen.

Do you see how the deepest belief in the cart showed up in all of these encounters? They were not only so busy hearing and seeing what they believed, but also they weren't believing what Jesus was telling them. They believed in the Messiah, but their partial belief caused them not to really *believe* the Messiah.

> John 12:16 (NASB): *These things His disciples did not understand at the first; but when Jesus was glorified, then they remembered that these*

*things were written of Him, and that they had
done these things to Him.*

Let's not dare think we are immune from reading, hearing, or seeing what we want to, what we've been taught, or what we've expected. We are all prone to pick and choose what suits us best, or fits our personal experiences. In truth, in this day and age with all of our technology, we have been programmed to hear with our eyes. I remember one speaking engagement I had when the Lord told me He wanted me to go in my sweats, no makeup, and my hair not done. I was challenged. He said He wanted me to be a parable. I had to start by having everyone check in with themselves. What were they experiencing with the appearance of something so unexpected? This is not how a speaker is supposed to present themselves! Were they offended? Had they tuned out? Had they already judged that nothing good would be shared? Or was their curiosity peaked and so they tuned in? How much do we miss because we only hear and see what we have been trained to hear and see? How often do we miss the truth right in front of us, thinking we believe when we don't even see clearly or have shut our ears from hearing?

The disciples believed Jesus was the Son of God by the works they witnessed Him doing, and they longed to do the same works.

> John 6:28-29 (NASB): *Therefore they said to Him, "What shall we do, so that we may work the works of God?" Jesus answered and said to them, "This is the work of God, that you believe in Him whom He has sent."*

What is it to really believe, according to Jesus – the kind of belief that leads to eternal life? We should get it right from the horse's mouth (sorry – I couldn't help myself with that one).

> John 3:31-36 (NASB): *"He who comes from above is above all, he who is of the earth is from the earth and speaks of the earth. He who comes from heaven is above all. What He has seen and heard, of that He testifies; and no one receives His testimony. He who has received His testimony has set his seal to this, that God is true.*

For He whom God has sent speaks the words of God; for He gives the Spirit without measure. The Father loves the Son and has given all things into His hand. He who believes in the Son has eternal life; but he who does not obey the Son will not see life, but the wrath of God abides on him."

Now this is fascinating. Jesus compares the one who 'believes' in the first half of this last sentence to the one who does not 'obey' in the second half. (Don't get tripped up by the 'wrath' of God – remember what we learned in the discussion on 'Love.')

Let's all put our thinking caps on. If we say we believe Jesus is the Son of God, yet we do not seek His counsel, His answers to our problems, His thoughts and responses about our situations, and we do not obey Him, *that* is telling. We are instructed to "pray without ceasing" (1 Thessalonians 5:17). This means we should be in constant communication with the Lord about every situation and encounter we face. Every single day we make hundreds of decisions, spill forth thousands of words, and choose numerous actions. If we believe Jesus is the Son of God, and we believe we have been chosen by Him to be about our Father's business, and we have 24/7/365 access to His wisdom and counsel but never, or rarely, seek His guidance, how deeply do we really believe any of those things? When He does give us His instruction or guidance and we do not obey, that is again telling. It may be saying we do not think God is good, benevolent, or for us although we do believe He exists. It may be saying we don't really believe Jesus is His Son. It may be saying we do not believe 'sonship' on our part includes obedience. It may indicate we have read the fullness of the writings we have been provided, but only see the ones which match our deepest belief about who Jesus *should* be and what our life with Him *should* look like. We only see in part because we have blocked His full disclosure with our expectations.

If you go through Jesus' life and His words with a 'yes/no' or 'agree/disagree' checklist, I would submit to you that you do not believe Jesus, though you may believe in all the facts about Him. Believing in Him as the Son of God looks like obedience to Him. How can you believe He is God and agree with some points He makes, but disagree with others? It requires an unconditional 'agree' with actions which follow all of what He has said, not our preferred verses. He says a lot in the written word which has been provided to us, but He also instructs each one of us personally. The two will never contradict each other. A perfect example of a personal instruction which also fits His model of teaching as demonstrated in the Bible is when He asked me to be a parable as I spoke to that group. It only had its impact by my obedience.

At the root of all our 'doing' is our 'believing.' Our 'believing' requires transformation, which is accomplished only by actively 'doing' things which align with what we now profess to believe. By obeying the One we confess to believe in, we intentionally apply our belief in practical ways. The belief we walk out turns knowledge into understanding. We now have legitimate experience because our demonstrated faith provided a platform for God to display His faithfulness to His Word.

The church today debates often about faith vs works (or what many call a "religious spirit"). To keep us real, we haven't progressed much from the conflicts that existed 2000 years ago.

James 2:18-20 (NASB): *But someone may well say, "You have faith and I have works; show me your faith without the works, and I will show you my faith by my works." You believe that God is one. You do well; the demons also believe, and shudder. But are you willing to recognize, you foolish fellow, that faith without works is useless?*

People believing they have to, or even can, earn their salvation by doing things or behaving a certain way is concerning. We are called instead to simply have faith in what Jesus has accomplished. Faith does please God. In fact, without it we are told it is impossible to please Him (Hebrews 11:6). Just because it is impossible to please God without faith, it does not say that it displeases Him to do works. The key is faith and works must be paired and in alignment. Works apart from faith is useless, but coming forth from faith they are powerful. Chapter 11 of Hebrews is completely about the phenomenal Old Covenant stalwarts of faith. When you peruse the accounts of their lives, you will see they took action which aligned with the instructions and promises they had received from God.

So, what does it look like to 'believe?' How does this new definition, understanding the full meaning and accurate intention of believing, change your emotional responses and choices in your daily activity?

"Come follow me," the Savior said.

AGREE + Submit

Prayer

Disciples are those who believe with follow-through. They 'walk the walk,' which cannot happen just from mental acquiescence to facts or information. The discipline required to do the work of believing flows from a deep acknowledgement and acceptance of God as God and of His Son as His one and only source given to us as the answer for everything we will ever need. We need discipline from Him and from within us to do this monumental work of believing. Let's look at 'discipline' next.

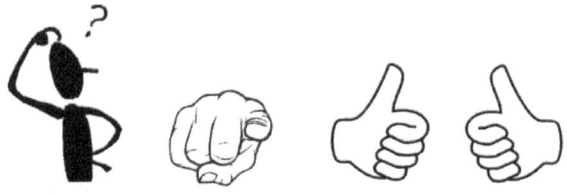

Discipline

Discipline is formative. What do you think of when you read the word 'discipline?' Do you remember scoldings, lists of rules requiring adherence, timeouts, endlessly chasing a carrot, mandated conformance, military-style order, structure, and regimen? Do you imagine an inner fortitude, grit, drive, will power, and determination? Is it compelled by 'shoulds,' 'oughts,' and 'have to's?' Is discipline external or internal for you?

I'm intrigued by the fact that I wrote the previous page a week ago, and since then have been stuck. I have not had any desire to write, nor have I known how exactly to proceed. This provides such a perfect illustration for the word 'discipline.' I am grateful for the pause.

In this world, we have been disciplined by schedules, time, deadlines, accomplishing goals, pushing ourselves to make things happen and get things done. We are trained to muster up an inner drive to produce (much that may not be what our Father wants produced). Our capital 'S' Self – our ego – has been programmed to feel good by doing.

Based on my worldly training, feeling stuck could induce a certain level of anxiety, possibly a sense of failure, compelling me to sit my-Self down and 'just do it.' What would come from that place would have a certain impact because flesh speaks to flesh, soul speaks to soul. I could inspire and motivate your activity by my very own activity, but I would be propagating a fleshly essence of discipline.

Romans 8:5-6 (NASB): *For those who are according to the flesh set their minds on the things of the flesh, but those who are according to the Spirit, the things of the Spirit. For the mind set on the flesh is death, but the mind set on the Spirit is life and peace,...*

The first couple of days during this past week I had the thought that I should be writing, yet there was no inspiration to do so. Finally, I simply submitted to the Lord, trusted Him to let me know when He was ready to work on 'discipline,' and I set it aside.

Today is Christmas Eve. I had today marked as a quiet day of reflection for myself. As I soaked in a hot bath, He began unveiling the week of inactivity, of not forcing the work. I have known this to be the 'discipline' of the Kingdom of Heaven, and laughed at the genius in the stalling out when I arrived at this specific word.

Zechariah 4:6 (NASB): *Then he said to me, "This is the word of the LORD to Zerubbabel saying, 'Not by might nor by power, but by My Spirit,' says the LORD of hosts.*

If we are going to communicate spirit-to-spirit, we must wait on the Spirit and not allow the flesh to hijack the work. Waiting on the Lord is an indispensable discipline for any disciple. Flesh will not change the world, and producing ever-increasing works compelled by flesh will not advance the Kingdom of Heaven, which comes by Spirit only. If you recall our discussion of 'Life,' you understand forging ahead to accomplish a work apart from His inspiration produces and increases death, not life.

It takes faith to wait – to wean the soul off its world-taught compulsion to produce and do and achieve and accomplish. Productivity in the Kingdom of Heaven comes from a completely different discipline than an internal mustering of Self-will to 'just do it.'

We have been indoctrinated with a theology that says, "God helps those who help themselves" when the gospel clearly teaches our Father knows we are helpless and comes to help us. He has always professed to be a help to His people (Isaiah 41:10-14). He loves to help, if we would be helpless! We are the ones who do not seem to know our own helplessness until He reveals it to us. Our Self will not be helpless apart from Him bringing us to it.

Romans 5:6-10 (NASB): *For while we were still helpless, at the right time Christ died for the ungodly. For one will hardly die for a righteous man; though perhaps for the good man someone would dare even to die. But God demonstrates His own love toward us, in that while we were yet sinners, Christ died for us. Much more then, having now been justified by His blood, we shall be saved from the wrath of God through Him. For if while we were enemies we were reconciled to God through the death of His Son, much more, having been reconciled, we shall be saved by His life.*

Revelation 3:17-21 (NASB): *Because you say, "I am rich, and have become wealthy, and have need of nothing," and you do not know that you are wretched and miserable and poor and blind and naked, I advise you to buy from Me gold refined by fire so that you may become rich, and white garments so that you may clothe yourself, and that the shame of your nakedness will not be revealed; and eye salve to anoint your eyes so that you may see. Those whom I love, I reprove and discipline; therefore be zealous and repent. Behold, I stand at the door and knock; if anyone hears My voice and opens the door, I will come in to him and will dine with him, and he with Me. He who overcomes, I will grant to him to sit down with Me on My throne, as I also overcame and sat down with My Father on His throne.*

A primary discipline for a disciple is to seek the Lord for the activity He intends for your life, both on a broad scale and in your moment-to-moment circumstances and interactions. Not only are you called to wait for the word of the Lord to come to you regarding your seeking, but also on the timing and activity of the Holy Spirit. The Holy Spirit's activity may come simultaneously with the word, or it may come separately. I have found the longer I walk with the Lord, the time frame between the word and the actual timing and Spirit-breathed inspiration increases. This is for the sake of disciplining my soul to wait in greater and greater measure.

What is the point of waiting? Waiting is training in how to abide in Him. It reduces the Self's need for control and answers, acknowledges His sovereignty, and diminishes ego-driven activities. It produces patience and brings us into rest. Waiting is part of the work of believing. In waiting, we discover the mystery of 'the fullness of time' (Galatians 4:4; Ephesians 1:9-11) through our micro experiences of it in our own life situations.

Studying what He has revealed of Himself to us in scriptures is another primary discipline of a disciple. Often through this discipline He speaks directly to us by His Spirit about the things we have been seeking. In fact, during our waiting, we must be disciplined in studying His word as part of hearing His answer. Often, greater insights precede the timing for any Spirit-initiated activity, and these insights frequently come to us from scriptural knowledge. Our study of scripture must be agenda-free as possible. Trust me, you can study in order to find loopholes for your-Self – flesh and soul – which is neither new nor uncommon to humanity. Jesus encountered it directly. Setting traps, finding loopholes, spying for ways to get our way and maintain the status quo of our soul is part of the games the flesh will play.

Luke 20:20 (NASB): *So they watched Him, and sent spies who pretended to be righteous, in order that they might catch Him in some statement, so that they could deliver Him to the rule and the authority of the governor.*

Check your soul's ambition and desire for the scriptures to conform to the comforts of the world. Be disciplined to seek truth in order to bring your-Self into alignment with and adherence to what the Spirit is saying. If it looks like, smells like, tastes like, feels like the world, it's the world. The Kingdom of Heaven smells like death to those who are dying, but life to those who are alive to Christ.

> **2 Corinthians 2:15-17** (NASB): *For we are a fragrance of Christ to God among those who are being saved and among those who are perishing; to the one an aroma from death to death, to the other an aroma from life to life. And who is adequate for these things? For we are not like many, peddling the word of God, but as from sincerity, but as from God, we speak in Christ in the sight of God.*

So what does 'discipline' in the Kingdom of God look like? How does this new definition, understanding the full meaning and accurate intention of discipline in our lives, change your emotional responses toward the discipline that comes from Him, and the self-discipline He desires us to develop?

pray.wait.trust.

They that wait upon the *Lord*
shall renew their strength;
they shall mount up with wings as eagles;
they shall run, and not be weary;
they shall walk, and not faint.
Isaiah 40:31

WAIT on THe LORD: Be OF GOOD COURAGe, AnD He SHALL STRenGTHen THIne HeART: WAIT, I SAY, On THe LORD. ~PSALm 27:14

ALL THE DAYS OF MY *appointed time* WILL I WAIT, ... *till* ...... MY CHANGE COME.
JOB 14:14

Disciples are disciplined. They hone their ears to hear, focus their eyes to see, and diligently seek the activity of

Heaven to disperse that activity here on earth. Only from the Spirit and the revealed truth of God, which we discover in part by studying scriptures, is this activity illuminated.

> John 4:23-24 (NASB): *But an hour is coming, and now is, when the true worshipers will worship the Father in spirit and truth; for such people the Father seeks to be His worshipers. God is spirit, and those who worship Him must worship in spirit and truth.*

Seeking spirit and truth is the discipline of a disciple and the hallmark of worshipers. It seems that learning about 'worship' is our next best place to go.

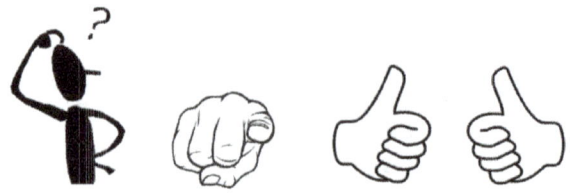

Worship

Can I get an 'Amen' and a 'Hallelujah?' What do you think of when you read the word 'worship?' Do you imagine gathering in a sacred place? Do you hear music and singing? Do you see arms raised and feet dancing, or solemn, reverent singing with hymnals in hand? Do you hear an organ or piano and choir, or a band-filled, spotlighted stage? Or is there more to it than that? What is your experience and expression?

Today's church culture has trained us to consider the pre-message period of our regularly scheduled weekly gathering as the time for 'praise and worship.' How has this limited us and made our 'worship' small? Has it framed our response of 'worship' within a construct of emotional ups and left us devoid of worship during any emotional downs? Are we emotionally affixed to a certain number of upbeat songs followed by a certain number of slow, solemn ones to feel 'worshipful?'

Let's look at what is at the heart of worship. Come with me into the wilderness of Judea. Listen to the final temptation exchange between Satan and Jesus.

Matthew 4:8-10 (NASB): *Again, the devil took Him to a very high mountain and showed Him all the kingdoms of the world and their glory; and he said to Him, "All these things I will give You, if You fall down and worship me." Then Jesus said to him, "Go, Satan! For it is written, 'YOU SHALL WORSHIP THE LORD YOUR GOD, AND SERVE HIM ONLY.'"*

Satan wasn't asking Jesus to go to a stone-constructed temple or synagogue and sing songs or dance for him. In context, he was asking Jesus to fall down prostrate before him. This action signified something more than a momentary posture. It contained within it the understanding of service to him. Jesus confirmed this in his response, 'You shall *worship* the Lord your God, *and serve* him only."

Worship is entirely about who we choose to serve. How rooted is our decision? Are we swayed by circumstances or our own logic, reasoning, or desires? In other words, do we worship our flesh?

Matthew 16:21-23 (NASB): *From that time Jesus began to show His disciples that He must go to Jerusalem, and suffer many things from the elders and chief priests and scribes, and be killed, and be raised up on the third day. Peter took Him aside and began to rebuke Him, saying, "God forbid it, Lord! This shall never happen to You." But He turned and said to Peter, "Get behind Me, Satan! You are a stumbling block to Me; for you are not setting your mind on God's interests, but man's."*

Wow! That's harsh! Jesus equates our service to our own interests as equivalent to serving Satan himself! At some level, we can believe there are three kingdoms: Light, darkness, and humanity. In truth, there are only two: Light and darkness. Our humanity serves one of these. Jesus' humanity was offered the same choice we are.

If we connect worship to positive, pleasurable happenings and emotions, what becomes of our worship in pain and suffering? If we turn our service moment-by-moment to the one who provides the pleasurable answer or result, we are not firmly established in the Kingdom of Heaven. If we turn from our service when pain and suffering arrives because our formula equates worship with pleasure only, we are not firmly established in the Kingdom of Heaven. Service implies obedience. If we determine to obey when it's easy and not when it costs us, we are not firmly established in the Kingdom of Heaven. We waver based on our pleasure and comfort, according to how the world has trained our flesh.

Let's look at some Biblical examples. Consider pain and suffering as a battle line drawn between the Kingdoms of Light and darkness; God tells Satan to consider Job.

> Job 1:8-12 (NASB): *The LORD said to Satan, "Have you considered My servant Job? For there is no one like him on the earth, a blameless and upright man, fearing God and turning away from evil." Then Satan answered the LORD, "Does Job fear God for nothing? Have You not made a hedge about him and his house and all that he has, on every side? You have blessed the work of his hands, and his possessions have increased in the land. But put forth Your hand now and touch all that he has; he will surely curse You to Your face." Then the LORD said to Satan, "Behold, all that he has is in your power, only do not put forth*

your hand on him." So Satan departed from the presence of the LORD.

Satan states his belief that the only reason Job worships God is because his life is blessed and nothing painful had touched him. This is a clear demonstration of why Jesus spoke against Satan when he showed up in Peter's flesh. We must be careful to recognize this belief in our own hearts and minds.

Satan proceeds to wreck Job's entire life. In one day, he destroys Job's house and kills all his children. How did Job respond?

Job 1:20-22 (NASB): *Then Job arose and tore his robe and shaved his head, and he fell to the ground and worshiped. He said,*

"Naked I came from my mother's womb,
And naked I shall return there.
The LORD gave and the LORD has taken away.
Blessed be the name of the LORD."

Through all this Job did not sin nor did he blame God.

He worshiped. He did not sin. His heart was blameless toward God.

Following that wreckage, Satan was permitted to remove Job's health, for he was convinced that if external suffering did not cause him to stop serving Light, physical pain and suffering would surely transfer him to the kingdom of darkness. God knew the depth of Job's integrity was great. While Job's wife was swayed by the suffering of her husband, Job remained steadfast.

> Job 2:9-10 (NASB): *Then his wife said to him, "Do you still hold fast your integrity? Curse God and die!" But he said to her, "You speak as one of the foolish women speaks. Shall we indeed accept good from God and not accept adversity?" In all this Job did not sin with his lips.*

Job's mouth did not waver in blessing God despite his circumstances. How often are the blessings which flow from our mouths situational?

> James 3:10 (NASB): *...from the same mouth come both blessing and cursing. My brethren, these things ought not to be this way.*

What about obeying hard instructions from the Lord? Do we assume God would never ask *us* to do 'such a thing' because our flesh does not agree with it? How can we know the depth of our own faith apart from it being tested? How can God exhibit the extent of His faithfulness apart from our willingness to obey His instructions which set the stage for Him? Abraham's faith stands as a model for us.

> Genesis 22:1-2 (NASB): *Now it came about after these things, that God tested Abraham, and said to him, "Abraham!" And he said, "Here I am." He said, "Take now your son, your only son, whom you love, Isaac, and go to the land of Moriah, and*

offer him there as a burnt offering on one of the mountains of which I will tell you."

Now, sacrificing children to the local gods was common practice at that time, so it may not have seemed like an outrageous request to Abraham from that perspective. However, Isaac had been a miracle child to Abraham and Sarah in their old age, with a promise he would be the inheritor of all Abraham owned, and through him God would fulfill his promise of innumerable offspring to Abraham. Would God ask such a thing? How do you respond when He requires you to sacrifice the promise He's given you?

Genesis 22:3-5 (NASB): *So Abraham rose early in the morning and saddled his donkey, and took two of his young men with him and Isaac his son; and he split wood for the burnt offering, and arose and went to the place of which God had told him. On the third day Abraham raised his eyes and saw the place from a distance. Abraham said to his young men, "Stay here with the donkey, and I and the lad will go over there; and we will worship and return to you."*

You worship with your immediate obedience, trusting He is faithful even when He is asking for something which does not seem to make sense.

Genesis 22:9-18 (NASB): *Then they came to the place of which God had told him; and Abraham built the altar there and arranged the wood, and bound his son Isaac and laid him on the altar, on top of the wood. Abraham stretched out his hand and took the knife to slay his son. But the angel of the LORD called to him from heaven and said, "Abraham, Abraham!" And he said, "Here I am." He said, "Do not stretch out your hand against the lad, and do nothing to him; for now I know that you fear God, since you have not withheld your son, your only son, from Me." Then Abraham raised his eyes and looked, and behold, behind him a ram caught in the thicket by his horns; and Abraham went and took the ram and offered him up for a burnt offering in the place* *of his son. Abraham called the name of that place The L*ORD *Will Provide, as it is said to this day, "In the mount of the L*ORD *it will be provided."*

*Then the angel of the L*ORD *called to Abraham a second time from heaven, and said, "By Myself I have sworn, declares the L*ORD*, because you have done this thing and have not withheld your son, your only son, indeed I will greatly bless you, and I will greatly multiply your seed as the stars of the heavens and as the sand which is on the seashore; and your seed shall possess the gate of their enemies. In your seed all the nations of the earth shall be blessed, because you have obeyed My voice."*

Hebrews 11:8-12, 17-19 (NASB): *By faith Abraham, when he was called, obeyed by going out to a place which he was to receive for an inheritance; and he went out, not knowing where he was going. By faith he lived as an alien in the land of promise, as in a foreign land, dwelling in tents with Isaac and Jacob, fellow heirs of the same promise; for he was looking for the city which has foundations, whose architect and builder is God. By faith even Sarah herself received ability to conceive, even beyond the proper time of life, since she considered Him faithful who had promised. Therefore there was born even of one man, and him as good as dead at that, as many descendants* AS THE STARS OF HEAVEN IN NUMBER, AND INNUMERABLE AS THE SAND WHICH IS BY THE SEASHORE.

By faith Abraham, when he was tested, offered up Isaac, and he who had received the promises was offering up his only begotten son; it was he to whom it was said, "IN ISAAC YOUR DESCENDANTS SHALL BE CALLED." He considered that God is able to raise people even from the dead, from which he also received him back as a type.

To be sure, I have shared examples under the old covenant. Post Jesus' sacrifice, we have the authority to rebuke every unseemly, adverse situation which dares approach our life, right? Actually, Jesus confirms we can expect tribulation in this world. We are not exempt from pain and suffering. Will we worship?

John 16:33 (NASB): *These things I have spoken to you, so that in Me you may have peace. In the world you have tribulation, but take courage; I have overcome the world.*

Jesus paid the price for us to be blessed and to have abundance. He paid the required sacrifice. He would never ask us to do something difficult or sacrificial, would He?

Matthew 19:16-22 (NASB): *[The Rich Young Ruler] And someone came to Him and said, "Teacher, what good thing shall I do that I may obtain eternal life?" And He said to him, "Why are you asking Me about what is good? There is only One who is good; but if you wish to enter into life, keep the commandments." Then he said to Him, "Which ones?" And Jesus said, "YOU SHALL NOT COMMIT MURDER; YOU SHALL NOT COMMIT ADULTERY; YOU SHALL NOT STEAL; YOU SHALL NOT BEAR FALSE WITNESS; HONOR YOUR FATHER AND MOTHER; and YOU SHALL LOVE YOUR NEIGHBOR AS YOURSELF." The young man said to Him, "All these things I have kept; what am I still* lacking?" Jesus said to him, "If you wish to be complete, go and sell your possessions and give to the poor, and you will have treasure in heaven; and come, follow Me." But when the young man heard this statement, he went away grieving; for he was one who owned much property.

Matthew 16:24 (NASB): *Then Jesus said to His disciples, "If anyone wishes to come after Me, he must deny himself, and take up his cross and follow Me.*

Romans 12:1 (NASB): *[Dedicated Service] Therefore I urge you, brethren, by the mercies of God, to present your bodies a living and holy sacrifice, acceptable to God, which is your spiritual service of worship.*

When our faith is tested, will we obey? Will we worship? Casting Crowns has recorded a couple of songs which express so beautifully a life of worship, which is a life lived as an affirmative response to God in this sacred, dusty temple regardless of any circumstance which touches our lives or our bodies (1 Corinthians 6:19-20).

Lifesong

Empty hands held high
Such small sacrifice
Now joined with my life
I sing in vain tonight
May the words I say
And the things I do
Make my lifesong sing
Bring a smile to you

Let my lifesong sing to you
Let my lifesong sing to you
I want to sign your name
To the end of this day
Lord led my heart was true
Let my lifesong sing to you

Lord I give my life
A living sacrifice
To reach a world in need
To be your hands and feet

So may the words I say

And the things I do

Make my lifesong sing

Bring a smile to you

Praise You In This Storm

I was sure by now, God you would have reached down

And wiped our tears away,

Stepped in and saved the day.

But once again, I say amen

That it's still raining

As the thunder rolls

I barely hear your whisper through the rain

"I'm with you"

And as your mercy falls

I raise my hands and praise

The God who gives and takes away

And I'll praise you in this storm

And I will lift my hands

That you are who you are

No matter where I am

And every tear I've cried

You hold in your hand

You never left my side

And though my heart is torn

I will praise you in this storm

I remember when I stumbled in the wind

You heard my cry you raised me up again

My strength is almost gone how can I carry on

If I can't find you

As the thunder rolls

I barely hear you whisper through the rain

"I'm with you"

I lift my eyes unto the hills

Where does my help come from?

My help comes from the Lord

The maker of heaven and earth

I lift my eyes unto the hills

Where does my help come from?

My help comes from the Lord

The maker of heaven and earth

And I'll praise you in this storm

And I will lift my hands

That you are who you are

No matter where I am

And every tear I've cried

You hold in your hand
You never left my side
And though my heart is torn
I will praise you in this storm

Worship is the whole of our lives – every response we have toward our Father in this dust suit He fashioned for us in this world of only two kingdoms. We worship in service to one or the other. Our choice determines if we will be formed for the Kingdom of Heaven.

Romans 5:3-5 (NASB): *And not only this, but we also exult in our tribulations, knowing that tribulation brings about perseverance; and perseverance, proven character; and proven character, hope; and hope does not disappoint, because the love of God has been poured out within our hearts through the Holy Spirit who was given to us.*

What does the depth of true 'worship' look like? How does this new definition, understanding the full meaning and accurate intention, expand your expressions of worship?

Here I Am, Send Me.

OH COME, LET US WORSHIP & BOW DOWN, Let Us KNEEL BEFORE THE LORD, OUR Maker!
PSALM 95:6

His kingdom will be
an everlasting kingdom,
and all rulers will
worship and obey Him
Daniel 7:27

"Go away SATAN,
The Scripture says
Worship the Lord your GOD
And serve only the Lord."

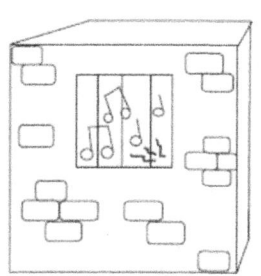

**Paul And Silas
In Jail**

Worship acknowledges God as God, trusting His goodness and sovereign capability to use everything for His perfect plans and purposes toward those who love Him and are called by Him to carry out His good pleasure (Romans 8:28). Nothing is wasted. He transmutes everything into a glorious, prosperous conclusion.

I think 'prosperity' is a good place to turn our attention next.

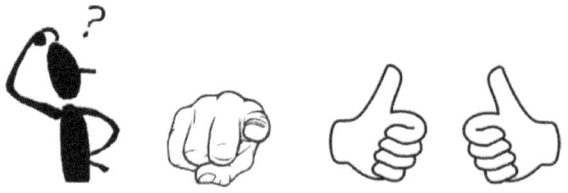

Prosperity

Cha-Ching! Show me the money! What do you see when you read the word 'prosperity?' Do you see dollar signs? Do memories of playing the board game Monopoly come to mind? Does travel to exotic places, images of mansions, or treasure chests full of sparkling jewels roll through your imagination?

A gospel anchored by God's desire and plan for the prosperity of His people has swept across capitalist American churches and disseminated around the globe. In fact, questions of faith have even been raised by some toward any believer who isn't experiencing a life of increasing possessions and affluence. An all-out effort should be made to pin point the problem in their walk with the Lord; something simply must not be right.

Wealth has become a measure by some of God's pleasure, though there is much in scripture which leaves that open. Wealth can be assigned to the wicked as well as the righteous, as a careful study reveals. The thoughts and intentions of the heart are ever the issue. I've witnessed leaders within the church waste precious time made available to them for advancing the gospel, or finding, feeding and healing the sheep. By running through calculations of how much Solomon's wealth would be worth in today's dollar, holding auction-style offerings which publicize the giving of each giver, or stirring up a frenzy to eliminate the debt ceiling of a church building, these leaders have neglected the debt ceiling most people carry in their unforgiving hearts.

I am not an advocate for a vow of poverty. In fact, I'm not an advocate of vows, period (Matthew 5:33-34). I do believe God definitely wants His children to be prosperous, but what does He mean? Let's see if we can unpack this a bit further than our pocket books and bank accounts lest it simply become mirrors and smokescreens for greed buried in our own hearts.

As an elder in the church, beloved Apostle John, mentions prosperity when he writes to one of his fellow believers.

> 3 John 2 (NASB): *Beloved, I pray that in all respects you may prosper and be in good health, just as your soul prospers.*

Do not miss the point that he stresses the prosperity of the soul as the benchmark for any other prosperity. The soul must prosper as the first priority. He listened well to his Master, Jesus.

> Matthew 16:26 (NASB): *For what will it profit a man if he gains the whole world and forfeits his soul? Or what will a man give in exchange for his soul?*

Matthew 6:33, then 25-32 (NASB): *But seek first His kingdom and His righteousness, and all these things will be added to you.*

"For this reason I say to you, do not be worried about your life, as to what you will eat or what you will drink; nor for your body, as to what you will put on. Is not life more than food, and the body more than clothing? Look at the birds of the air, that they do not sow, nor reap nor gather into barns, and yet your heavenly Father feeds them. Are you not worth much more than they? And who of you by being worried can add a single hour to his life? And why are you worried about clothing? Observe how the lilies of the field grow; they do not toil nor do they spin, yet I say to you that not even Solomon in all his glory clothed himself like one of these. But if God so clothes the grass of the field, which is alive today and tomorrow is thrown into the furnace, will He not much more clothe you? You of little faith! Do not worry then, saying, 'What will we eat?' or 'What will we drink?' or 'What will we wear for clothing?' For the Gentiles eagerly seek all these

things; for your heavenly Father knows that you need all these things.

Jesus places seeking God's kingdom and righteousness above even our basic provisional needs of food and clothing. He gets to the core of our faith in God as a good Father who knows we have these basic needs with a faithfulness to meet them. In this exchange, He also limits the provision to meeting these basic needs. He doesn't address an exhaustive list of wants. Skillful marketers expand our needs in our minds by convincing us we need (or deserve) what we truly only want. As soon as we believe something is a 'need' for our survival, it becomes embedded in our fight-or-flight survival mechanism. Very crafty of marketers, huh?

John, along with his fellow disciples, were ones who left everything to follow Jesus at His invitation. Others were invited. We are invited. Let's look at His invitation to the rich young ruler who asked Jesus how to acquire eternal life. Though Jesus points him to the commandments, the ruler knew something was still lacking.

Matthew 19:20-22 (NASB): *The young man said to Him, "All these things I have kept; what am I still lacking?" Jesus said to him, "If you wish to be complete, go and sell your possessions and give to the poor, and you will have treasure in heaven; and come, follow Me." But when the young man heard this statement, he went away grieving; for he was one who owned much property.*

I find it fascinating that Jesus expresses this as necessary to 'be complete.' He also indicates that treasure in heaven is acquired by divesting ourselves of our possessions here on earth. The disciples heard this exchange and Peter questioned Jesus about what they would receive, as ones who accepted His invitation.

Matthew 19:27-29 (NASB): *Then Peter said to Him, "Behold, we have left everything and followed You; what then will there be for us?" And Jesus said to them, "Truly I say to you, that you who have followed Me, in the regeneration when the Son of Man will sit on His glorious throne, you also shall sit upon twelve thrones,*

judging the twelve tribes of Israel. And everyone
who has left houses or brothers or sisters or
father or mother or children or farms for My
name's sake, will receive many times as much,
and will inherit eternal life.

The disciples accepted Jesus' invitation to follow Him in the 'regeneration' and would be greatly rewarded. Keep in mind most of them died as martyrs, so we must rightly interpret both the type and timing of this reward. Part of 'regeneration' is being reprogrammed to operate under a different Kingdom. The economy of the Kingdom of Heaven is not based on money or ownership. Apart from releasing all this world offers and has taught, they would not be capable of rightly judging from the perspective of Heaven. The same is true for us. We use our worldly measures and filters in our decisions and judgments. Our attitudes toward wealth and its use is likely the greatest test we face. By divesting ourselves of the things of this world, we untangle ourselves from what we've known and step outside of the world's systems. It may be the first time we have ever seen clearly. We must be able to see in order to rightly judge. By following Jesus in the 'regeneration,' the disciples' sight was prepared. In fact, Jesus connects clear vision with attitudes toward wealth.

> Matthew 6:22-24 (NASB): *"The eye is the lamp of the body; so then if your eye is clear, your whole body will be full of light. But if your eye is bad, your whole body will be full of darkness. If then the light that is in you is darkness, how great is the darkness!*
>
> *"No one can serve two masters; for either he will hate the one and love the other, or he will be devoted to one and despise the other. You cannot serve God and wealth.*

When Jesus taught His disciples to pray, He instructed them to pray that God's Kingdom would come and His will would be done here on earth as it is in Heaven (Matthew 6:9-13). Jesus came to earth to show us what that looks like. If He brought the prosperity of heaven to earth, what does it look like? We have no record of Him acquiring possessions here on earth for Himself.

Luke 9:57-58 (NASB): *[Exacting Discipleship] As they were going along the road, someone said to Him, "I will follow You wherever You go." And Jesus said to him, "The foxes have holes and the birds of the air have nests, but the Son of Man has nowhere to lay His head."*

Matthew 6:19-21 (NASB): *"Do not store up for yourselves treasures on earth, where moth and rust destroy, and where thieves break in and steal. But store up for yourselves treasures in heaven, where neither moth nor rust destroys, and where thieves do not break in or steal; for where your treasure is, there your heart will be also.*

Jesus did not walk through the byways of Israel handing out money, did He? He brought the compassion of Heaven to provide for the practical needs of broken, hurting people in a broken, hurting world. Money wasn't required to accomplish His work then, and it's not required to accomplish it now through us. Is it possible that money gets in our way? As long as we have money to rely upon (or we believe in its necessity), we won't access the supernatural power available to us. He did not need money to feed thousands of people. He did not need money to pay medical, counseling, or funeral costs for countless individuals. He did not need to earn money to meet his tax obligations to the ruling government. Everything was freely available to Him and through Him. He had authority over all of it. And honestly, if we truly tapped into the power He made available to us, we would wreak havoc on the economy. Evidently, we believe more in money and medicine than in the "It is finished" declaration from the cross and the released Holy Spirit power of Pentecost. If the Kingdom of Heaven has come, and things are freely available through Jesus, and we began freely giving what we have freely received, people would be healed and fed at no cost in the same way Jesus provided for needs. Apple carts would be overturned everywhere and people would know Jesus is alive in His Body! Every need would be freely met.

Isaiah 55:1-5 (NASB):

"Ho! Every one who thirsts, come to the waters;
And you who have no money come, buy and
eat.
Come, buy wine and milk
Without money and without cost.
"Why do you spend money for what is not
bread,
And your wages for what does not satisfy?
Listen carefully to Me, and eat what is good,
And delight yourself in abundance.
"Incline your ear and come to Me.
Listen, that you may live;
And I will make an everlasting covenant with
you,
According to the faithful mercies shown to
David.
"Behold, I have made him a witness to the
peoples,
A leader and commander for the peoples.
"Behold, you will call a nation you do not know,
And a nation which knows you not will run to
you,
Because of the LORD your God, even the Holy

One of Israel;

For He has glorified you."

We can only experience certain facets of the Lord when we reach this point of need. Only by being needy can we experience aspects of humanity and the world. These experiences illumine us and grant wisdom we cannot gain in any other way. The Apostle Paul gained a contentment which few will choose to know. This wisdom is necessary to inform right judgements.

Philippians 4:11-13 (NASB): *Not that I speak from want, for I have learned to be content in whatever circumstances I am. I know how to get along with humble means, and I also know how to live in prosperity; in any and every circumstance I have learned the secret of being filled and going hungry, both of having abundance and suffering need. I can do all things through Him who strengthens me.*

1 Timothy 6:6-7 (NASB): *But godliness actually is a means of great gain when accompanied by contentment. For we have brought nothing into the world, so we cannot take anything out of it either.*

So what does prosperity in the Kingdom of Heaven look like? How does this new definition, understanding the full meaning and accurate intention of the prosperity He desires for us, change your perspective and emotional responses you have toward what you have in your life?

Everything is free when people have true freedom. Let's explore that next.

Freedom

What do you see when you read the word 'freedom?' Here in the United States of America, we just celebrated the 4th of July – considered our Independence Day. It's fascinating to me that I began writing this chapter six months ago, and never got past the lyrics of the song (below). Unbeknownst to me, there were areas I had not experienced freedom yet that would provide insights for this chapter. Freedom is a fascinating undertaking. We have many misconceived notions of what it is and what it's for.

There was a song written in 1967, sung by Andy Williams, called "Born Free." It's recently been re-recorded by Kid Rock. What do you think of when you read the word 'freedom?' Do you think of shackles coming off and being let go from slavery or prison? Do you think of the pursuit of happiness? Do you think of "We The People" and the Bill of Rights?

Let's consider the lyrics to that song:

Born Free

Born free, as free as the wind blows
As free as the grass grows
Born free to follow your heart

Live free and beauty surrounds you
The world still astounds you
Each time you look at a star

Stay free, where no walls divide you
You're free as the roaring tide
So there's no need to hide

Born free, and life is worth living
But only worth living
'cause you're born free

Are we born free? I guess that depends on what 'free' means to you. If you think in terms of 'independence,' then the answer would be "No." In actuality, we are born utterly needy, helpless, and dependent, are we not? We are formed and fashioned by the socioeconomic parameters, religious or non-religious standards, and cultural norms that surround us as we grow up. And yet, inside of us is an aspiration to be 'independent' which we reckon as freedom. We push and press against restraints, demand our rights, and agitate the very atmosphere around us with our clamoring for independent, self-sufficiency. For those who the 'standards' have not worked in their favor, that is an attempt to break out of the confinement of their upbringing. For others who the 'standards' have been favorable, independence is an attempt to make everyone else conform to the defined standards so they can remain 'free.' Somehow, our idea of 'unity' has been twisted to force conformity of agreement to establish 'rightness.' So, what is it to be 'free?'

Realizing the truth we were created to be bond servants helps. We are always bond servants. The question is, to what? We have only one choice available to us, though we believe we have endless choices. In reality, we have one choice between two kingdoms: Light or darkness. Life or death. Blessing or curse. Every subsequent choice available to us exists within the kingdom we choose.

Let's begin with darkness. This world we are born into is this kingdom. The entire world construct has been formed and fashioned by the prince of this world who was given dominion of it at the first disobedience. Consider that. Disobedience to the Source of Light, Life, and Blessing makes way for the reign of darkness. We are born as bond servants in the earth's darkness in our humanity. We perceive the darkness as light because we can see it, touch it, smell it, taste it, and hear it with our natural senses. But it remains darkness.

God chose to hide a mystery of Light in secret darkness. It is Christ in you, the hope of glory (Colossians 1:27). This glory is covered in darkness and must be perceived apart from our natural senses. It is a glory which can only be discerned spiritually. Can you see it in you? Do you realize it is working to advance the Light in you and recalibrate what you believed to be light that was darkness? Do you comprehend that it invites you to become a bond servant to Light instead of darkness? It is God's divine nature seeded in you that desires to circumcise all the dark workings, mental constructs, and misidentities attached to you by this world and return you to the simple relationship of an innocent child with a loving Father.

The ultimate freedom is freedom from all unbelief and every fear which hinders perfect, Divine, unconditional agape love flowing through us perpetually. We are free to choose to have every hindrance to love torn down inside of us, or to obstruct its flow by believing the darkness is Light.

Yet 'dark forces' operate all around us. The Bible clearly states until Jesus returns to establish His reign here on earth, these forces will remain. What we don't consider is that darkness operates in us to the extent we have not allowed Light to eradicate it. Proverbs 16:2 tells us that man thinks his ways are clean and pure in his own estimation, but God looks at the motives. In the Amplified translation, it actually says, "God weighs the spirits." Our motivations have 'spiritual forces' attached to them so that any word or action coming forth from us will have those spirits released with them, whether dark or light. The Father is the only Source of Light, so obedience to Him as our motivation attaches Light to our words and actions. When we choose not to seek and obey, but lean on our own worldly-acquired understanding, even our 'good' deeds propelled from the motivations of our own heart release darkness (Jeremiah 17:9), continuing the dominion which was established at the first disobedience.

Being a bond servant to Love is expressed in obedience. After all, if you believe the Father is the purest Source of

Love, Blessing, Life (all things benevolent), then any request He makes or instruction He gives is for the highest good. Again, if you believe this, obedience is simple, and the circumcision of darkness happens in the discomfort of the process. The discomfort of the process can lead us to believe we are being mistreated, as we press for that illusion of 'independence' if we haven't reframed our understanding of the work being accomplished. Disobedience is evidence of unbelief that God is the purest Source of Love, Blessing, Life (all things benevolent), and the darkness we cling to is actually light (which it is not).

The greatest demonstration of our choice to be bond servants to Light will be evidenced by the use of every good and perfect gift given to us by the Father in service to the Kingdom of Heaven for the benefit of others. Our pushing and pressing against restraints, demanding our rights, and agitating the very atmosphere around us with our clamoring for independent, self-sufficiency will cease. We will only do what we see the Father doing, and only say what we hear the Father saying. This place of unity can truly exist; the place where every individual earnestly seeks the thoughts, words, and activity of the Father for them with the intention of obedience. We have weaned our soul to be still and utterly dependent on the Source of our bondage. You are not free to be something until you are free to be nothing. As soon as you are utterly submitted to Him being Who He chooses to be in and through you, you are free. The mystery in you is visible.

> Colossians 3:3-5 (NASB): *For you have died and your life is hidden with Christ in God. When Christ, who is our life, is revealed, then you also will be revealed with Him in glory.*
>
> *Therefore consider the members of your earthly body as dead to immorality, impurity, passion, evil desire, and greed, which amounts to idolatry.*

You have heard it said in the world 'we live to fight another day,' but the Word instructs us to 'die and hide in Christ.'

So what does freedom really look like? When do our hearts soar? When they fully operate the way they were designed at full capacity of our gifts for the advancement of the Kingdom of Heaven and in the service of bringing others into their true identity. How does this new definition, understanding the full meaning and accurate intention of His freedom, change your perspective or expectations for being free?

But we have this treasure in earthen vessels, that the excellency of the power may be of God, and not of us.

2 Corinthians 4:7

Storing Up

Treasure In Heaven

Luke 12:34

For where your treasure is, there will your heart be also

This circumcision of darkness for greater Light is eloquently expressed by Jesus in terms of 'bearing fruit' in John's gospel account:

John 15:1-8 (NASB): *[Jesus Is the Vine – Followers Are Branches] "I am the true vine, and My Father is the vinedresser. Every branch in Me that does not bear fruit, He takes away; and every branch that bears fruit, He prunes it so that it may bear more fruit. You are already clean because of the word which I have spoken to you. Abide in Me, and I in you. As the branch cannot bear fruit of itself unless it abides in the vine, so neither can you unless you abide in Me. I am the vine, you are the branches; he who abides in Me and I in him, he bears much fruit, for apart from Me you can do nothing. If anyone does not abide in Me, he is thrown away as a branch and dries up; and they gather them, and cast them into the fire and they are burned. If you abide in Me, and My words abide in you, ask whatever you wish, and it will be done for you. My Father is glorified by this, that you bear much fruit, and so prove to be My disciples.*

Thus, our next thing to explore is fruit.

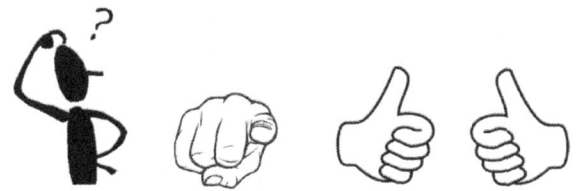

Fruit

How often have you heard someone say, "You will know them by their fruit."? What do you see when you read the word 'fruit?' What comes to your mind? What is the 'fruit' you are watching for?

Do you have images of helping the poor, serving the homeless, going on missions, caring for the elderly? Do you look for service in the church, scripture memorization, prayer meetings, living a 'clean-cut' life, having a steady career and stable finances?

Or do you think about the addict, the thief, the adulterer, or the excessively affluent? What about the divorced or the bankrupt? What constitutes good 'fruit' and what constitutes bad 'fruit'?

When you consider the statement, "You will know them by their fruit" was actually made by the Lord Jesus Christ, it makes sense that it would be best to hear His own expression about what 'fruit' represents. Otherwise, we are trapped in assessing and analyzing behaviors which have nothing to do with the actual teachings of Jesus, but are simply the traditions of man which are often focused on behavior modification. We miss the mark entirely with that focus.

Let's consider the context of the gospel accounts where Jesus actually makes this statement.

Matthew 7:15-20 (NASB): *[A Tree and Its Fruit] Beware of the false prophets, who come to you in sheep's clothing, but inwardly are ravenous wolves. You will know them by their fruits. Grapes are not gathered from thorn bushes nor figs from thistles, are they? So every good tree bears good fruit, but the bad tree bears bad fruit. A good tree cannot produce bad fruit, nor can a bad tree produce good fruit. Every tree that does not bear good fruit is cut down and thrown into the fire. So then, you will know them by their fruits.*

Matthew 12:33-37 (NASB): *[Words Reveal Character] "Either make the tree good and its fruit good, or make the tree bad and its fruit bad; for the tree is known by its fruit. You brood of vipers, how can you, being evil, speak what is good? For the mouth speaks out of that which fills the heart. The good man brings out of his good treasure what is good; and the evil man brings out of his evil treasure what is evil. But I tell you that every careless word that people speak, they shall give an accounting for it in the day of judgment. For by your words you will be justified, and by your words you will be condemned."*

Luke 6:39-45 (NASB): *And He also spoke a parable to them: "A blind man cannot guide a blind man, can he? Will they not both fall into a pit? A pupil is not above his teacher; but everyone, after he has been fully trained, will be like his teacher. Why do you look at the speck that is in your brother's eye, but do not notice the log that is in your own eye? You hypocrite, first take the log out of your own eye, and then you will see clearly to take out the speck that is in your brother's eye. For there is no good tree which produces bad fruit, nor, on the other hand, a bad tree which produces good fruit. For each tree is known by its own fruit. For men do not gather figs from thorns, nor do they pick grapes from a briar bush. The good man out of the good treasure of his heart brings forth what is good; and the evil man out of the evil treasure brings forth what is evil; for his mouth speaks from that which fills his heart.*

If you look at the context of all three of these gospel passages which give account of this expression by Jesus, all three refer to spoken words that come out of a person's mouth as an overflow of what abundantly exists, or fills up, their heart. Whether this is referencing false prophets who prophesy out of the deception of their own heart (Jeremiah 23:25-27), those who speak with flattering lips and a double heart (Psalm 12:2), those who speak proudly (Psalm 17:10), those who speak peace deceptively because evil is really in their hearts (Psalm 28:3), those who gather information about the thoughts, words, or deeds of one to go whisper it to others (Psalm 41:6, Proverbs 26:18-28), those speaking oppression, revolt, or lies (Isaiah 59:13), or those who speak truth in their hearts (Psalm 15:2), those filled with the Holy Spirit speaking to one another in psalms, hymns, spiritual songs, and giving thanks (Ephesians 5:19-20), and those speaking gospel-based exhortations (1 Thessalonians 2:3-5), Jesus clearly points to the words we speak that originate from the heart as 'fruit.'

So if words are the fruit we are looking for, but the motivations of the heart are compelling those words, how can we assess the fruit? This is extremely challenging. Consistent, observable discrepancies or cognitive dissonance between words and actions might provide some indication, but every individual is in various stages of growth and maturity in working out the Truth revealed to their heart by the Lord. The reality is our best place of 'fruit' assessment is ourselves. We should be concerned with our 'fruit' crop, since we will be answerable for it to God. We won't answer for anyone else. We should heed Paul's admonishment to test ourselves.

> 2 Corinthians 13:5 (AMPC): *Examine and test and evaluate your own selves to see whether you are holding to your faith and showing the proper fruits of it. Test and prove yourselves [not Christ]. Do you not yourselves realize and know*

[thoroughly by an ever-increasing experience] that Jesus Christ is in you – unless you are [counterfeits] disapproved on trial and rejected?

In many ways, our preoccupation with analyzing anyone else's 'fruit' is a tactic to avoid investigating our own, and as a means of measuring ourselves against false standards to feel good about ourselves. We have only one standard – the perfect Lamb of God. Try to measure yourself against anything or anyone else to prop yourself up and you will meet His Standard face-to-face for clarity. That's the 'fruit crop' standard to test yourself against. Read and study His words and actions with the understanding of His heart. Read His nice words. Read His harsh words. Read His words to His Father. Read His words to His disciples. Read His words to His antagonists. Observe His actions in the multitude of situations recorded for us.

Jesus never spoke anything which wasn't truth. He didn't flatter. He didn't mince words. He was always kind, but not always nice. He loved perfectly with honesty and truth at all times. He called forth destiny by correcting and rebuking what needed to be cut away. He pointed

out what wasn't acceptable in the Kingdom of Heaven –
competitiveness, ambition, lording it over others,
retribution, excess, indifference, self-concern, worldly
focus, etc. His actions perfectly matched His words.
When we test them in our own hearts we know them to
be truth. Perfect 'fruit.'

Proverbs 18:20-21 (NASB): *With the fruit of a
man's mouth his stomach will be satisfied;
He will be satisfied with the product of his lips.
Death and life are in the power of the tongue,
And those who love it will eat its fruit.*

Death and Life. Those who love 'death' will love to eat its
fruit. Those who love 'life' will love to eat its fruit. What
we consider to be words of life which are not compelled
by intentions of life are actually death. The Lord sees the
heart of a person bringing forth those words. What we
consider to be words of death not compelled by
intentions of life are death. Regardless if we would
consider them to be words of life or death, *all* words
compelled by intentions of life, are truly life. Jesus' harsh
words were just as life-giving as his kind, gentle words.

Jesus didn't posture with a lot of hot air. He didn't talk the talk. He walked out and lived out His message. He calls those who are His to learn from Him and follow His example.

> Ephesians 5:6-10 (NASB): *Let no one deceive you with empty words, for because of these things the wrath of God comes upon the sons of disobedience. Therefore do not be partakers with them; for you were formerly darkness, but now you are Light in the Lord; walk as children of Light (for the fruit of the Light consists in all goodness and righteousness and truth), trying to learn what is pleasing to the Lord.*

Understanding the abundance of our heart is the determining factor of our 'fruit,' and we were formerly darkness, how do we transform the motivations in our heart? Jesus insured we would have everything we would need for that transformation.

John 14:26 (NASB): *But the Helper, the Holy Spirit, whom the Father will send in My name, He will teach you all things, and bring to your remembrance all that I said to you.*

The Holy Spirit was sent to remind them, and us, of what Jesus spoke. His words are his 'fruit' from a heart full of, thus compelled by, the Holy Spirit. The 'fruit' we speak is produced from 'fruit' in our hearts, and the Holy Spirit cultivates the 'fruit' which pleases the Lord. Galatians 5:22-23 tells us this fruit is love, joy, peace, patience, kindness, goodness, faithfulness, meekness, and self-control.

Do not miss the point. The Holy Spirit is working to fill our hearts to capacity with these, which enables us to maintain these things internally regardless of what is occurring externally. As the fruit grows and matures within, our heart responses will not waiver based on circumstances without. We will be established and no longer tossed to and fro in our emotional responses and behavioral reactions, but will have an abundance of 'fruit' in our hearts with which to nourish others. We have already looked extensively at 'Love.' Let's get an accurate glimpse of the others.

I want to start by pointing out in The One New Man Bible translation, which is rich in Hebrew roots, the passage in Galatians does not separate each of the fruits with a comma, but rather has three clusters of three 'fruit' separated by a comma: "...love joy peace, patience kindness goodness, faithfulness gentleness self-control..." indicating the connected meanings between the three in each cluster. The three 'fruits' in each cluster seem to be the process, or progression of evidenced maturity, within that cluster.

Cluster 1

Love

Review the extensive previous discussion on 'Love.'

Page 35

> Colossians 3:14 (AMPC): *And above all these (virtues) [put on] love and enfold yourselves with the bond of perfectness [which binds everything together completely in ideal harmony].*

Joy

The word translated 'joy' is the Greek word 'chara' which means joy, gladness, rejoicing, cause of joy, occasion of rejoicing, or bliss, specifically because it recognizes the utter sufficiency of the grace of God. It would be easy to think that pleasant causes and occasions are what give rise to joy. However, consider that it was the 'joy' set before Jesus that enabled Him to endure the cross. In Mark's gospel account, we read at the conclusion of the Seder meal Jesus has with his disciples as His last meal before His death, they conclude by singing. The Seder tradition concludes with the singing of what the Hebrew refer to as 'the Hallel,' which is Psalm 113-118. I encourage you to read these Psalms in light of what Jesus knew was set before Him. Two of the final six verses of the Hallel state:

Psalm 118:24,29 (The One New Man Bible): *This is the day that the LORD has made! We will rejoice enthusiastically and be glad in it!*

O give thanks to the LORD, for He is good: for His loving kindness endures forever.

Jesus sang this as truth from His heart on His way to His betrayal, scourging, and crucifixion. When you read all of the Hallel Psalms as they would have been sung that night, you experience His own comprehension of the will of His Father awaiting His accomplishment. Notice the enthusiastic rejoicing and the enduring loving kindness. Accomplishing His Father's will brought Him joy! This joy was independent of any 'pleasurable' experience. The same is true for us. God's grace is always sufficient for the accomplishment of His will. Therefore, we can always rejoice and be glad in every circumstance aligned with His plans and purposes. In part, His plans and purpose includes producing 'fruit' in us. The experience of that process is not always pleasurable.

Peace

The word translated 'peace' is the Greek word 'eirēnē' which means tranquility, concord (friendship and peace between people and countries), unity, love of peace, every kind of blessing and good., or benediction. Yet Jesus, the Prince of Peace, tells us He didn't come to bring peace to the earth, but a sword (Matthew 10:34-36). Jesus also distinguishes the peacemakers as ones who will be called sons of God. How do we make sense of this?

A false 'peace' is propped up with 'false' words and actions from a heart which loves death. Being a peacekeeper for comfort's sake is vastly different from being a peacemaker who will speak honestly and truthfully for the sake of life. The sword Jesus brings is one to circumcise and cut away the death-bearing false peace which brings no true unity with Him and the Father, and therefore with no one else. If peace is a lie, it isn't His peace. Lying peace produces counterfeit relationships established in false love, and therefore a fabricated unity. When the inner fitfulness of our hearts attempts to create peace with dishonest words and actions, we no longer have undisturbed tranquility in our souls, which is the peace of Jesus. This is not the peace of Jesus. Jesus' words and actions are always an honest revelation of what His heart knows to be true. They match.

Where Jesus' heart contains no deception, ours are deceitful. As the true peace 'fruit' of the Holy Spirit grows and matures, our deceptive words and actions diminish, and truth-speaking, peacemaking flourishes.

Matthew 5:9 (AMPC): *Blessed (enjoying enviable happiness, spiritually prosperous – with life-joy and satisfaction in God's favor and salvation, regardless of their outward conditions) are the makers and maintainers of peace, for they shall be called the sons of God!*

Cluster 2

Patience

The word translated 'patience' is the Greek word 'makrothumia' which means patient enduring of evil, fortitude, slowness of avenging injuries, clemency, long-suffering, forbearance (the ability to be polite, calm, and patient in difficult situations), and patient expectation. How often do we recognize we need 'forbearance,' which is really only the threshold of the deeper, wider, longer, and broader fullness of Holy Spirit produced patience? Imagine patiently enduring evil and being slow to avenge injuries. Hebrews 12:24 tells us Jesus' blood is better than Abel's, speaking a better word for mercy, forgiveness, and reconciliation instead of crying for vengeance.

Consider a heart which is abundant in its desire for mercy, forgiveness, and reconciliation; a heart which contains no desire for vengeance, but only blessing. The Holy Spirit wants to produce this 'patience' fruit in our hearts. That's vastly greater than an ability to make it through the day without honking and yelling at anyone in traffic, or giving a sharp response to a child or spouse due to being tired at the end of a long day. What would it be like for 'patience' to become a natural flow that requires no focus or effort? The Holy Spirit wants to grow and mature this divinely-regulated characteristic in us to such a degree we are infused with it for every situation we face; that we may be changed from short-tempered to long-tempered. We are invited to participate in cultivating this crop.

Colossians 1:9-12 (NASB): *For this reason also, since the day we heard of it [the Colossians' love in the Spirit], we have not ceased to pray for you and to ask that you may be filled with the knowledge of His will in all spiritual wisdom and understanding, so that you will walk in a manner worthy of the Lord, to please Him in all respects, bearing fruit in every good work and increasing in the knowledge of God; strengthened with all power, according to his glorious might, for the attaining of all steadfastness and patience; joyously giving thanks to the Father, who has qualified us to share in the inheritance of the saints in Light.*

Kindness

The word translated 'kindness' is the Greek word 'chrēstotēs' which means well-fit for use (for what is really needed), kindness which is also serviceable, useful kindness which refers to meeting real needs in God's way and timing, and kindness that meets the need and avoids human harshness or cruelty. It conveys the idea of being adaptable to others.

Kindness is not sugary 'southern hospitality' dripping with pleasantness and niceties. It's practical. It's personal. It's specific to tangible individual needs. It usually costs something. Kindness is demonstrated by not harshly requiring everyone else to adapt to our personal needs or considering ourselves better and more deserving, but by striving to become adaptable to the needs of those around us. We begin to look for ways to be different or change for the benefit of someone else. Consider the cost of God's kindness to meet the need we had for redemption and reconciliation to Him as our Father. Empty words which say good things from a heart that loves death cannot bring forth this 'fruit.' James explains this empty faith as follows:

> James 2:15-17 (NASB): *If a brother or sister is without clothing and in need of daily food, and one of you says to them, "Go in peace, be warmed and be filled," and yet you do not give them what is necessary for their body, what use is that? Even so faith, if it has no works, is dead, being by itself.*

Living faith which brings life from the heart will have actions that align with the words. Saying all the right things apart from meeting the practical needs is cruel and does not demonstrate the love of God and His concern for the provision of our needs. If He has blessed us with the capability and means to meet another's needs, and we offer niceties and platitudes while leaving them in need, this Holy Spirit 'fruit' of kindness needs to be nurtured and developed in our hearts.

Most importantly, Holy Spirit 'kindness' does not meet needs haphazardly. It is orchestrated to move in God's way and in His timing. This mandates a relationship seeking to connect to the heart of God in each and every situation. Institutionalizing a program cannot be compared with the specific, individual, and unique way God wants to accomplish his provision for maximum benefit in a person's life. Our hearts have to be filled by the Holy Spirit with this divine level of concern and intentionality toward people, or we risk turning them into an empty reporting mechanism on the bottom-line of our program.

Goodness

The word most frequently translated 'goodness' comes from the Greek word 'agathōsynē' which means generosity, and uprightness of heart and life. Notice the connection of 'heart' and 'life.' This goodness flows naturally from a heart which is compelled by life – not death.

I would venture to guess most people connect 'generosity' to finances. I think we need to look more deeply at this concept so we are not limited in our understanding. Let's begin by getting a glimpse of God's generosity to us through the gifts of the Holy Spirit and the ministries of Jesus.

> 1 Corinthians 12:4-11 (NASB): *Now there are varieties of gifts, but the same Spirit. And there are varieties of ministries, and the same Lord. There are varieties of effects, but the same God who works all things in all persons. But to each one is given the manifestation of the Spirit for the common good. For to one is given the word of wisdom through the Spirit, and to another the word of knowledge according to the same Spirit; to another faith by the same Spirit, and to another the effecting of miracles, and to another prophecy, and to another the distinguishing of spirits, to another various kinds of tongues, and to another the interpretation of tongues. But one and the same Spirit works all these things, distributing to each one individually just as He wills.*

This is a lot of gifts, ministries, and effects! Do not miss these are all for the *common good.* We each are given something (or some things), but not all things. However, we have all of these gifts given for our good through one another. For this to happen, we must be *generous with the gifts we've been given.*

> Ephesians 2:10 (NASB): *For we are His workmanship, created in Christ Jesus for good works, which God prepared beforehand so that we would walk in them.*

God planned good works for us to do in advance of our creation in Christ, and He generously gave us everything we would require to effect (accomplish) those works by lavishing us with the unique gifts of the Holy Spirit selected for our particular good works. Our goodness is being generous with the gifts we have been given for the benefit of others. It's light and easy. The only time we run into trouble is when we get the notion we somehow earned or merited the gifts, or they are evidence of our own goodness, or our gifts are somehow more (or less) valuable than any of the others, or we think they are to be used for our own gain instead of lavished on others – for the common good.

We have already seen that meeting practical needs is 'kindness,' so financial generosity is by no means excluded. However, the fuller understanding of 'goodness' is the vast opportunity we have to be generous with our very selves – all the resources of our lives, such as our gifts, time, prayers, connections – everything which benefits the greater common good for God's glory. This de-personalizes the abundance God has given us individually as being for us or for our sole ownership. The abundance is community property and a direct effect of the good works God prepared for us and equipped us to do in our new creation in Christ.

Cluster 3

Faithfulness

The word translated 'faithfulness' is the Greek word 'pistis' which means good faith, honesty, integrity, assurance, fidelity, and truthfulness.

Faithfulness is the essence of a faith which fully aligns words and actions with what it says it believes. This progressive work begins with the initial ability to believe in Truth which came as a free gift to us by grace. This actionable faith is a reasonable mental acknowledgement. Like a switch, your faith is flipped on in your brain to believe what it didn't believe before, and thus you begin to see and understand things differently. This is true of every believer.

The outworking of the faith of every believer is then accomplished through the work of renewing our minds. This renewal is accomplished by tearing down old-man (dead) patterns of emotions, thinking, and behaviors which sustained and supported what we used to believe – the ways we sustained our lives apart from faith in God. This realignment is our taking on the essence of our full faith – faithfulness. It requires we build new structures of emotional responses, thought patterns, and behaviors which match what we profess to now believe. This realignment moves from a mental nod of agreeing with what Jesus said, to practically applying what He said to our specific life circumstances and fully embracing and putting on our new-man. This work of reconstruction can be messy, because renovation is just that. Again, this Holy Spirit work is the 'fruit' to be developed in every believer. The Holy Spirit's objective is for us to have the same faith in God which He has in Himself.

> Romans 3:3-4 (NASB): *What then? If some did not believe, their unbelief will not nullify the faithfulness of God, will it? May it never be! Rather, let God be found true, though every man be found a liar, as it is written,*
>
> *"THAT YOU MAY BE JUSTIFIED IN YOUR WORDS, AND PREVAIL WHEN YOU ARE JUDGED."*

The establishment of that faith-ful-essence is the goal.

Some believers have been given the 'gift of faith' by the Holy Spirit. This gift is an empowerment to 'move mountains' through their prayers and simple obedience, whether they are aware of it or not. Hebrews 11 tells us of many with this gift of faith. By this Spirit-given gift, a believer has extraordinary confidence in God's promises, power, and presence so they can take heroic stands for the future of God's work in the church. This strong and unshakeable confidence in God, His Word, and His promises enables them to do extraordinary, superhuman things. As with all spiritual gifts, the gift of faith is given to some believers whose use of it edifies and inspires others in the Body of Christ.

> Hebrews 11:4-12 (NASB): *By faith Abel offered to God a better sacrifice than Cain, through which he obtained the testimony that he was righteous, God testifying about his gifts, and through faith, though he is dead, he still speaks. By faith Enoch was taken up so that he would not see death; AND HE WAS NOT FOUND BECAUSE GOD TOOK HIM UP; for he obtained the witness that before his being taken up he was pleasing to God. And without fait it is impossible to please Him, for he who comes to God must believe that He is and that He is a rewarder of those who seek Him. By faith Noah, being warned by God about things not yet seen, in reverence prepared an ark for the salvation of his household, by which he condemned the world, and became an heir of the righteousness which is according to faith.*
>
> *By faith Abraham, when he was called, obeyed by boing out to a place which he was to receive for*

an inheritance; and he went out, not knowing where he was going. By faith he lived as an alien in the land of promise, as in a foreign land, dwelling in tents with Isaac and Jacob, fellow heirs of the same promise; for he was looking for the city which has foundations, whose architect and builder is God. By faith even Sarah herself received ability to conceive, even beyond the proper time of life, since she considered him faithful who had promised. Therefore there was born even of one man, and him as good as dead at that, as many descendants AS THE STARS OF HEAVEN IN NUMBER, AND INNUMERABLE AS THE SAND WHICH IS BY THE SEASHORE.

And there are more in Hebrews 11 who were given the gift of faith under the Old Covenant, to inspire us in the development of our faith-ful-essence in the New Covenant.

Meekness

The word translated 'meekness' is the Greek word 'prautēs' which means gentleness and mildness, with the underlying idea of patience and kindness from Cluster 2. Again, meekness is a progression that is producing fruit, more fruit, and much fruit (John 15:1-8).

I don't know what you think of when you read the words 'meekness' and 'gentleness,' but I have always had an image of a mousy, quiet, timid woman (probably because I'm a woman), sitting 'prim and proper,' with her hands in her lap and her legs crossed at her ankles. She's nothing but polite.

Well, it's time to shake up that notion. Are you ready?

One of the most beautiful and powerful creatures is the horse. Their powerfulness in the wild is breathtaking, but that power is not useful. For it to be useful, it must be harnessed and directed. This power-harnessing training, in Old English terms, is known as 'meeking' the horse. Through a rigorous process, this powerful animal is broken to the point of making it submit to having a bit – a foreign, hard piece of metal – put in its mouth to lead its every movement. What appears to be a harsh process (and it can be depending on how much the horse fights against it), actually creates a pliable and teachable spirit, making it more powerful and useful to its master.

A 'meeked' horse is one which can be led into war because its rider knows it will heed every subtle signal without wavering. The great race horse – in the gate, at the ready to yield the fullness of its power under the direction of its rider at the very instant the gate opens for its release is shaped through 'meeking'. A wild, 'unmeeked' horse is beautiful, and powerful, but not useful.

The process of creating a still, gentle, submission to the Master within us is the same. To be powerfully useful in His hands requires that we will not buck, stomp, or kick against His leading. We yield all of ourselves to Him, as it pleases Him. His choice. A meek person is not a weak person, but a controlled person.

Matthew 5:5 (AMPC): *Blessed (happy, blithesome, joyous, spiritually prosperous – with life-joy and satisfaction in God's favor and salvation, regardless of their outward conditions) are the meek (the mild, patient, long-suffering), for they shall inherit the earth!*

The 'meeked' are the inheritors of the earth because they have been broken to yield their power only at the signal of their Master. They have been made useful for His purposes. They have learned to bring their will, character, and opinions, no matter how strong, under control.

Self-Control

The word translated 'self-control' is the Greek word 'enkrateia' which means temperance (moderation) and continence (voluntary control and self-restraint) which is the ability to completely moderate and govern yourself according to God's thoughts and ways. Imagine our 'meeked' horse being so trained to know and heed its master's movements that the bit is no longer required.

This Holy Spirit 'fruit' is produced by constant reliance on and communication with the Master until you are able to discern His thoughts, emotions, and movement in each situation instead of some formulaic or systematic approach to life. All patterns are obliterated. You moderate yourself to remain submitted and under His control. This mastery over your entire personality allows Him to choose the facet of His personality He wants to manifest through you in every circumstance for the most beneficial outcome of every individual.

Interestingly, in the Old Testament 'self-control' does not show up because the Holy Spirit was not poured out for the 'meeking' process necessary to produce this fruit. The lack of the 'meeking' process for the production of this fruit is still evident today.

> 2 Timothy 3:2-5 (NASB): *For men will be lovers of self, lovers of money, boastful, arrogant, revilers, disobedient to parents, ungrateful, unholy, unloving, irreconcilable, malicious gossips, without self-control, brutal, haters of good, treacherous, reckless, conceited, lovers of pleasure rather than lovers of God, holding to a form of godliness, although they have denied its power; Avoid such men as these.*

The lack of self-control is evidence of resistance to being 'meeked' by the Holy Spirit, and the results are evident in both the words and motivations – 'fruit' – and the associated actions of unbelief which flow from the fullness of that resistant heart. Their deepest motivations all relate to self-love, whether it is connected to the love of money, arrogance, or being ungrateful. Their words and actions expose their unbelief: boasting, disobedience, gossiping, despising good, recklessness, and pleasure seeking.

Whether an individual has not received the gift of the Holy Spirit that is available, or is resisting the 'meeking' process by the Holy Spirt which they have received, the result is the same. Of course, we can never forget the 'fruit' producing work of the Holy Spirit is a process which takes place over time. We, however, get to choose if we will quench the Spirit or cooperate with that process.

Jesus' life is the perfect exhibit of perfect 'fruit.' The Holy Spirit is diligently working in sync with the Father's heart to orchestrate situations in our lives which provide opportunities to multiply this fruit in us.

So, what does 'fruit' in the Kingdom really look like? What are we assessing? Who are we assessing? How does this new definition, understanding the full meaning and accurate intention of His desire for fruit in our lives, change what you are evaluating?

Remember, this is a work between the Holy Spirit and each individual separately for the unique good works planned and purposed by God for that person for the common good. We must assess and test our own fruit. The Apostle Paul exhorts us to make it our ambition to lead a quiet life and attend to our own business (1 Thessalonians 4:11).

Colossians 3:12-17 (NASB): *So, as those who have been chosen by God, holy and beloved, put on a heart of compassion, kindness, humility, gentleness and patience; bearing with one another, and forgiving each other, whoever has a complaint against anyone; just as the Lord forgave you, so also should you. Beyond all these things put on love, which is the perfect bond of unity. Let the peace of Christ rule in your hearts, to which indeed you were called in one body; and be thankful. Let the word of Christ richly dwell within you, with all wisdom teaching and admonishing one another with psalms and hymns and spiritual songs, singing with thankfulness in your hearts to God. Whatever you do in word or deed, do all in the name of the*

Lord Jesus, giving thanks through Him to God the Father.

Blessed are the meek, for they will inherit the earth. Matthew 5:5

Jesus

patience
gentleness
kindness
joy
love
self control
goodness
peace
meekness

All of this fabulous, divine 'fruit' is produced in us by the Holy Spirit, which must mean it is 'holy' fruit. Let's turn our attention to Holiness and see what we discover.

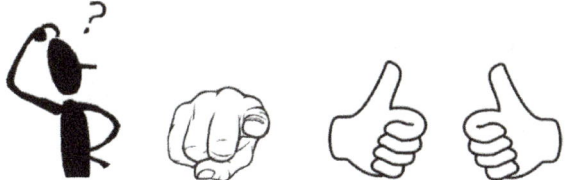

Holiness

When you read the word 'holiness,' what do you see? What images or concepts flash before your mind? Do you see a "Perfect 10" scorecard, a superior anointing of the Holy Spirit, halo-adorned saints of a high stature and purity, or an intimate knowledge of the scriptures?

Holiness is important to God. He cannot be anything other than holy, and because He created us in His likeness, He's looking for Himself in us. Numerous times in the Old Covenant God expresses His standard of holiness for His people, Israel.

> Leviticus 20:26 (NASB): *Thus you are to be holy to me, for I the Lord am holy; and I have set you apart from the peoples to be Mine.*

In the King James Version, it says:

> *And ye shall be holy unto me: for I the LORD am holy, and have severed you from other people, that ye should be mine.*

What does holiness mean? What does God's holiness look like? How can He expect it from us? How do we become holy? If we are not holy based on our understanding, do we just need to "squeeze harder" to produce it? Can we even produce it? We've got some questions to answer, so let's get started.

The Hebrew "qadowsh" is the word for "holy" used in this verse. Qadowsh means sacred, holy, Holy One, saint, and set apart. It comes from the root word "qadash" which means to consecrate, sanctify, prepare, dedicate, be hallowed, be holy, be sanctified, be separate.

Leviticus 20:26 states exactly this: set apart, or severed. In a sense, Israel was circumcised, or cut away, from other peoples.

Let's not lose sight here of who did the separating. Israel did not separate themselves, but were set apart by the Lord Himself. We see this in other instances in the Old Testament as well. He separated Isaac from Ishmael and Jacob from Esau for the promised seed. He separated Joseph from his brothers for His pre-ordained plan to save His people from famine. He separated Moses from his family and people in preparation to deliver Israel from bondage in Egypt. These are just a few. There was Noah, Abram and Sarai, Gideon and his 300, David, Samson, and many others. God makes choices and separates one from another for His purposes.

When we turn to the New Covenant, we hear Jesus stating the choosing is done by Him. Again, selection and appointments are made by the Godhead, in accordance with the will of the Father.

> John 15:16 (NASB): *You did not choose Me but I chose you, and appointed you that you would go and bear fruit, and that your fruit would remain, so that whatever you ask of the Father in My name He may give to you.*

> Ephesians 1:11-12 (NASB): *[In Him] also we have obtained an inheritance, having been predestined according to His purpose who works all things after the counsel of His will, to the end that we who were the first to hope in Christ would be to the praise of His glory.*

Let's explore the two different Greek root words in the New Testament for "holiness": "hosiotēs" and "hagiōsynē."

Hosiotēs only appears twice (Luke 1:72-75 and Ephesians 4:20-25), and means piety and sacred observance of all duties to God. The passage in Ephesians specifically connects holiness back to God's likeness.

> But you did not learn Christ in this way, if indeed you have heard Him and have been taught in Him, just as truth is in Jesus, that, in reference to your former manner of life, you lay aside the old self, which is being corrupted in accordance with the lusts of deceit, and that you be renewed in the spirit of your mind, and put on the new self, which in the likeness of God had been created in righteousness and holiness of the truth.
>
> Therefore, laying aside falsehood, SPEAK TRUTH EACH ONE of you WITH HIS NEIGHBOR, for we are members of one another. (NASB)

Hagiōsynē is the root of every other occurrence of holiness in the New Testament and relates to sanctity and sanctification. This root word (hagios) is used for the Holy Spirit – the Spirit by which we are sanctified.

The Holy Spirit, the very Spirit of God, is the generating source of God's holiness. Everything the Holy Spirit directs is holy because it can be nothing other.

Let's consider God and all of His activity to see if we can gain a clearer meaning of holiness to direct our understanding.

God always does what He says He will do. His actions, regardless of how they may look to us, always align with the good, loving, and beneficial intentions of His heart.

> Psalm 93:5 (NASB): *Your testimonies are fully confirmed: Holiness befits Your house, O LORD, forevermore.*

He is 100%, fully committed to His intention. In His fierce commitment, He will adjust His actions to align with His intention in order to foster a better result, or response from His people. We must not mistake this as anything apart from His holiness. No shifting shadow is in Him; His intentions and purposes never change (James 1:17). His methods of achieving them do. We must learn not to focus on His actions and "behaviors" according to our own limited understanding, and often our own preferences for comfort and pleasure.

Interestingly, God regrets things He has done (Genesis 6:6) but He does not repent – change His mind or intention (Numbers 23:19). The reasons in His heart and mind for any actions He takes are always holy, good, benevolent, and rooted in His essence of love. He never does anything which violates His own will or nature.

God is always truthful. He clearly expresses His emotions, desires, purposes, blessings, displeasures, consequences, expectations, etc. He doesn't intimidate, manipulate, or use deceptive means to accomplish compliance to His will. No pretense, flattery, or preferential treatment exists in His relations.

He wants to see Himself in us – holy as He is holy. When do we know we've arrived? The moment we are "chosen" is the very moment we become holy, not by anything we do, but because the One who IS holy chose to set us apart and appoint us for plans and purposes of His choosing. We participate in our own sanctification by submitting to the Holy Spirit's leading, just as Jesus did. He learned obedience to the Holy Spirit, and we follow in His footsteps.

Romans 12:1 (NASB): *[Dedicated Service] Therefore I urge you, brethren, by the mercies of God, to present your bodies a living and holy sacrifice, acceptable to God, which is your spiritual service of worship.*

Ephesians 1:3-6 (NASB): *Blessed be the God and Father of our Lord Jesus Christ, who has blessed us with every spiritual blessing in the heavenly places in Christ, just as He chose us in Him before the foundation of the world, that we would be holy and blameless before Him. In love He predestined us to adoption as sons through Jesus Christ to Himself, according to the kind intention of His will, to the praise of the glory of His grace, which He freely bestowed on us in the Beloved.*

Colossians 3:12-14 (NASB): *So, as those who have been chosen of God, holy and beloved, put on a heart of compassion, kindness, humility, gentleness, and patience; bearing with one another, and forgiving each other, whoever has a complaint against anyone; just as the Lord forgave you, so also should you. Beyond all these things put on love, which is the perfect bond of unity.*

2 Timothy 1:8-11 (NASB): *Therefore do not be ashamed of the testimony of our Lord or of me His prisoner, but join with me in suffering for the gospel according to the power of God, who has saved us and called us with a holy calling, not according to our works, but according to His own purpose and grace which was granted us in Christ Jesus from all eternity, but now has been revealed by the appearing of our Savior Christ Jesus, who abolished death and brought life and immortality to light through the gospel, for which I was appointed a preacher and an apostle and a teacher.*

Hebrews 5:8 (NASB): *Although He was a Son, He learned obedience from the things which He suffered.*

1 Peter 1:14-16 (NASB): *As obedient children, do not be conformed to the former lusts which were yours in your ignorance, but like the Holy One who called you, be holy yourselves also in all your behavior because it is written, "YOU SHALL BE HOLY, FOR I AM HOLY."*

Because the Holy Spirit is Holy, submission and obedience to the Holy Spirit is our holiness. Participating in this sanctifying work, we share in the way Jesus walked out His life as a human in this world.

Luke 4:1-2a (NASB): *[The Temptation of Jesus] Jesus, full of the Holy Spirit, returned from the Jordan and was led around by the Spirit in the wilderness for forty days, being tempted by the devil.*

Romans 8:14 (NASB): *For all who are being led by the spirit of God, these are sons of God.*

Galatians 5:18 (NASB): *But if you are led by the Spirit, you are not under the Law.*

The Holy Spirit is available to us without measure, limited only by our own unwillingness to seek His counsel moment-by-moment and submit to His instructions. We are holy because The Holy One chose us, and we perfect holiness by participating in the development of our holiness through practice. Grace covers the mistakes.

2 Corinthians 7:1 (NASB): *[Paul Reveals His Heart] Therefore, having these promises, beloved, let us cleanse ourselves from all defilement of flesh and spirit, perfecting holiness in the fear of God.*

1 Thessalonians 3:11-13 (NASB): *Now may our God and Father Himself and Jesus our Lord direct our way to you; and may the Lord cause you to increase and abound in love for one another, and for all people, just as we also do for you; so that He may establish your hearts without blame in*

holiness before our God and Father at the coming of our Lord Jesus with all His saints.

Hebrews 12:9-11 (NASB): *Furthermore, we had earthly fathers to discipline us, and we respected them; shall we not much rather be subject to the Father of spirits, and live? For they disciplined us for a short time as seemed best to them, but He disciplines us for our good, so that we may share His holiness. All discipline for the moment seems not to be joyful, but sorrowful; yet to those who have been trained by it, afterwards it yields the peaceful fruit of righteousness.*

With our brother, Jesus, as our perfect model, we can see what holiness looks like. Jesus often awoke and sought solitude with the Father and the Holy Spirit. He was continually led by the Holy Spirit, only doing what He saw the Father doing and saying what He heard the Father saying. Jesus demonstrated holiness as this diligent and intentional seeking the Holy Spirit's counsel and following the guidance received. It's as simple as "Listen. Obey. Repeat." He will guide us straight out of our self-constructed life and into the good plans and purposes for which we were chosen.

If we truly believe His intentions for ourselves and others are always from His essence of love, and if we want to love Him with all our heart, soul, mind and strength, and our neighbors as ourselves, then intentional obedience to such holiness is only logical. By default our obedience is the expression of receiving His love for us and others. We have been chosen and set apart for such pure and perfect love. He planned this work in us and through us from the foundations of the world. This unfathomable gift of access to the very heart and mind of God for our little moment-by-moment lives is our inheritance. Seeking the Holy Spirit's guidance in every situation we face brings God's highest and best into this world.

Our hunger and search for righteousness has been satisfied with the gift of the Holy Spirit. Now we must decide how often we "open" that gift, freely receive and freely give God's answers in this life.

So what does holiness really look like? How is it acquired? How does this new definition, understanding the full meaning and accurate intention of His desire for holiness in our lives, change your emotional responses about it and efforts to produce it?

Because of the Holy Spirit, we are able to receive God's judgment in our lives now – today. Let's look at that interesting thought next.

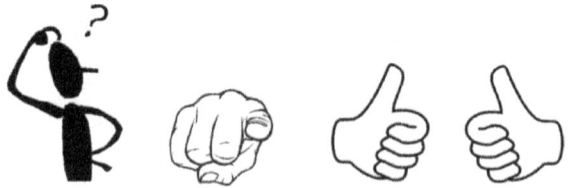

Judgment

When you read the word 'judgment,' what do you see? Do you imagine a particular day with an angry judge and panel of jurors, a balancing scale of 'rights' and 'wrongs,' the hammer of justice dropping with a 'guilty' verdict, or fire and brimstone destruction?

Let's start with the hilarity of the fact there is no clear agreement on how to even spell this word. Internet space is littered with discussions on whether it is 'Judgement' or 'Judgment.' It appears the answer is 'yes' to both. That's quite a paradox.

I am fascinated how the writing of this chapter coincides with the confirmation hearings for Brett Kavanaugh as nominee for a new Supreme Court Judge here in the United States of America. The questions and scrutiny undertaken is evidence of how critical the ability to judge well truly is.

The Bible – in both the Old and New Testament – has a lot to say about judgment. Moses, heeding the advice of Jethro, his father-in-law, was the first person noted to put a judicial hierarchy in place to decide matters between people according to the Law given on Mount Sinai (Exodus 18). Different levels of leaders were given different levels of judicial oversight. There's even an entire book in the Old Testament called "Judges." In the New Testament, we are told by Paul we, as followers of Jesus Christ, will play a monumental role as judges.

> 1 Corinthians 6:3 (NASB): *Do you not know that we will judge angels? How much more matters of this life?*

What does judgment, or judging, entail? What is the purpose and necessity for it? The primary function of judgment is ruling over matters and rendering a decision or reaching a conclusion. Typically judgment is necessary when there are conflicting opinions, differing perspectives, or a wrong has occurred according to an agreed-upon standard, contract, or a law. No wonder the Bible has much to say about judges, judging, and judgment. Think about it, we make judgments every single day with every decision we make between conflicting options available to us. Our decision-making abilities are the same thing as making judgments for our lives. With every individual making individual judgments for their lives, there's 100% likelihood of conflicts which need sorting out.

In order to judge in any situation, it requires an understanding of all the facts, any ruling previously made over a similar case which has established a precedent, and consequences and impact of any decision rendered. All of these must be considered and weighed in order to insure the best outcome. For most people, a primary concern is justice is done.

Isaiah 9:6-7 (NASB):

For a child will be born to us, a son will be given to us;
And the government will rest on His shoulders;
And His name will be called Wonderful
Counselor, Mighty God, Eternal Father, Prince of Peace.
There will be no end to the increase of His
government or of peace,
On the throne of David and over his kingdom,
To establish it and to uphold it with justice and righteousness
From then on and forevermore.
The zeal of the LORD of host will accomplish this.

Let's consider a couple of important 'judgments' made in the Old Testament, one by King David and the other by his son, King Solomon.

Let's look at David first. In 2 Samuel 12, we read about how Nathan the prophet was sent by the Lord to tell David a parable about how a rich man with an abundance of resources took from a poor man the only lamb which belonged to his family. David, being enraged, judged this rich man worthy of death. Nathan then showed David how his judgment should be impartially applied to his own actions with Bethsheba and her husband, Uriah. He was like the rich man of abundant resources taking from the poor man. The ability to judge impartially is very important, and yet difficult to do with ourselves.

When David's son, Solomon, had taken the throne, he was presented with a difficult case between two women who became mothers out of wedlock. We read about his judgement of this case in 1 Kings 3:16-28. The argument between these mothers was that one woman's child died during the night as she slept and rolled over onto him. As the other woman slept, she switched her dead child with the living child. Since there were no witnesses, it was one woman's word against the other. It's not like they had DNA testing back then! Solomon had to employ wisdom of maternal instincts and nature to determine who the real mother of the living child was, so he ordered the living child be split in two and divided between the women. They each could have half of the child, when in reality both of the children would be dead. The true mother's desire for her child to live was greater than having him for herself, so she cried out for the other woman to have him. Solomon was able to make an accurate judgment and render justice by giving the living child to the true mother. As important as impartiality, God-granted Wisdom is required to get to the truth of a matter to insure judgments are justly made. Solomon was granted this Wisdom because he requested it above honor and glory, riches and possessions, or revenge against enemies, and a long life for himself.

As you can see, judgment and justice are closely related. Well, what exactly does justice look like? It depends on the justice system you are under. Different systems of law exist for different citizens, situations, or types of offenses. I'm most familiar with basic civil and criminal law, common law, admiralty law, martial law, and military law. Each justice system has its own mechanisms and means of evaluating and rendering judgments. We must remember judgments are not strictly punitive, but can also include remuneration, restoration, and rewards.

Interestingly, we find different justice systems in terms of spiritual matters as well. First, the ruler of this world lives, who himself has been judged but brings accusations based on his justice system, with its hierarchy of thrown-down angels and rulers of demons.

Matthew 12:24-27 (NASB): *But when the Pharisees heard this, they said, "This man casts out demons only by Beelzebul the ruler of the demons."*

And knowing their thoughts Jesus said to them, "Any kingdom divided against itself is laid waste; and any city or house divided against itself will not stand. If Satan casts out Satan, he is divided against himself; how then will his kingdom stand? If I by Beelzebul cast out demons, by who do your sons cast them out? For this reason they will be your judges.

John 8:44 (NASB): *You are of your father the devil, and you want to do the desires of your father. He was a murderer from the beginning, and does not stand in the truth because there is no truth in him. Whenever he speaks a lie, he speaks from his own nature, for he is a liar and the father of lies.*

John 16:8-11 (NASB): *And He [the Helper], when He comes, will convict the world concerning sin and righteousness and judgment; concerning sin, because they do not believe in Me; and concerning righteousness, because I go to the Father and you no longer see Me; and concerning judgment, because the ruler of this world has been judged.*

Revelation 12:9-10 (NASB): *And the great dragon was thrown down, the serpent of old who is called the devil and Satan, who deceives the whole world; he was thrown down to the earth, and his angels were thrown down with him.*

Then I heard a loud voice in heaven, saying,

"Now the salvation, and the power, and the kingdom of our God and the authority of His Christ have come, for the accuser of our brethren

has been thrown down, he who accuses them
before our God day and night.

Second, there is the system of Law given to Moses, together with all the Old Testament prophets.

Matthew 11:13 (NASB): *For all the prophets and the Law prophesied until John.*

John 5:44-45 (NASB): *How can you believe, when you receive glory from one another and you do not seek the glory that is from the one and only God? Do not think that I will accuse you before the Father; the one who accuses you is Moses, in whom you have set your hope.*

Acts 15:1,5 (NASB): *[The Council at Jerusalem] Some men came down from Judea and began teaching the brethren, "Unless you are circumcised according to the custom of Moses, you cannot be saved." ...But some of the sect of*

*the Pharisees who had believed stood up, saying,
"It is necessary to circumcise them and to direct
them to observe the Law of Moses."*

Third, there is the system declared and revealed in the gospel of the Father's love and His Son's atonement.

Luke 16:16 (NASB): *"The Law and the Prophets
were proclaimed until John; since that time the
gospel of the kingdom of God has been
preached, and everyone is forcing his way into it.*

John 1:16-18 (NASB): *For of His fullness we have
all received, and grace upon grace.*

*For the Law was given through Moses; grace and
truth were realized through Jesus Christ. No one
has seen God at any time; the only begotten God
who is in the bosom of the Father, He has
explained Him.*

Acts 13:38-41 (NASB): *Therefore let it be known to you, brethren, that through Him forgiveness of sins is proclaimed to you, and through Him everyone who believes is freed from all things, from which you could not be freed through the Law of Moses. Therefore take heed so that the thing spoken of in the Prophets may not come upon you:*

'BEHOLD, YOU SCOFFERS, AND MARVEL, AND PERISH;

FOR I AM ACCOMPLISHING A WORK IN YOUR DAYS,

A WORK WHICH YOU WILL NEVER BELIEVE, THOUGH SOMEONE SHOULD DESCRIBE IT TO YOU.'"

Here's the amazing thing: we each get to choose the spiritual justice system by which we are judged. We actually get to decide who our judge will be. Is that as simple as making your request known? Well, no. Here's an easy way to think of it: justice is "just as." The justice system you fall under is not based on what you want to receive, but is "just as" you give. You demonstrate your choice by how you deal with others.

Matthew 7:1-2 (NASB): *[Judging Others] "Do not judge so that you will not be judged. For in the way you judge, you will be judged; and by your standard of measure, it will be measured to you.*

Luke 6:36-37 (NASB): *Be merciful, just as your Father is merciful.*

"Do not judge, and you will not be judged; and do not condemn, and you will not be condemned; pardon, and you will be pardoned.

John 3:17-19 (NASB): *For God did not send the Son into the world to judge the world, but that the world might be saved through Him. He who believes in Him is not judged; he who does not believe has been judged already, because he has not believed in the name of the only begotten Son of God. This is the judgement, that the Light has come into the world, and men loved the darkness rather than the Light, for their deeds were evil.*

John 5:22-23 (NASB): *For not even the Father judges anyone, but He has given all judgment to the Son, so that all will honor the Son even as they honor the Father. He who does not honor the Son does not honor the Father who sent Him.*

Romans 11:32 (NASB): *For God has shut up all in disobedience so that He may show mercy to all.*

Not only do we get to decide which justice system we want to be judged by, but also we do not have to wait until some future date for one gigantic, monumental hearing. We have access to the throne of God perpetually. We have the counsel of God the Father by His Holy Spirit who can give us the Father's decision (ruling, judgment) for every situation in our lives. We can seek Him without ceasing and follow His decisions, living under His judgment now – today. After all, judgment is about weighing all the facts, reaching a conclusion, and rendering a decision. The Father sees everything and knows what we cannot know. By applying His judgments for our lives and to every situation we face, we demonstrate that we trust Him. We also live with a peaceful conscience.

2 Corinthians 13:5 (NASB): *Test yourselves to see if you are in the faith; examine yourselves! Or do you not recognize this about yourselves, that Jesus Christ is in you – unless indeed you fail the test?*

Hebrews 3:7-9 (NASB): *Therefore, just as the Holy Spirit says,*

"TODAY IF YOU HEAR HIS VOICE,

DO NOT HARDEN YOUR HEARTS AS WHEN THEY PROVOKED ME,

AS IN THE DAY OF TRAIL IN THE WILDERNESS,

WHERE YOUR FATHERS TRIED Me BY TESTING Me,

AND SAW MY WORKS FOR FORTY YEARS.

So what does judgment and justice really look like in the Kingdom of God? How does this new definition, understanding the full meaning and accurate intention of His justice and judgments, change your perspective and emotional responses to His activity of justice and judgment in your life and the world?

When God's just and righteous judgments are enforced, then all things are reconciled to the Father (Colossians 1:19-20). Getting clear about 'reconciliation' seems to be where we are headed next.

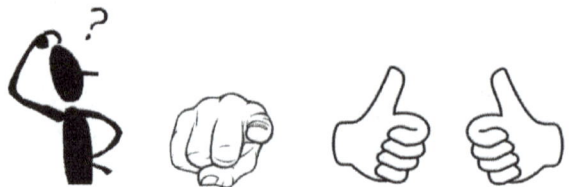

Reconciliation

When you read the word 'reconciliation,' what do you see? Do you see mediation and conflict resolution sessions, concessions of mutual compromise for the sake of win-win agreements, kumbaya group hugs, or reconnecting hearts and lives to walk in unity?

THE COMMENCEMENT OF A GROUP HUG

Be RECONCILED
Be RECONNECTED

We all have lots of things in our lives which can be, or should be, reconciled. We experience a much greater peace in our lives when things are properly reconciled, don't we?

The word 'reconcile' occurs nine times in the New Testament, but there are four distinct Greek root words with varying definitions depending on the context of reconciliation. We need to piece those words and contexts together if we are going to understand the Biblical idea of reconciliation.

The first Greek root word is 'diallassomai' which means to be reconciled to another. Jesus gives instruction in Matthew 5:23-25 before leaving your gift at the altar. Notice He does not speak to you having something against your brother, but rather being aware when another has something against you.

> Matthew 5:23-25 (NASB): *Therefore if you are presenting your offering at the altar, and there remember that your brother has something against you, leave your offering there before the altar and go; first be reconciled to your brother, and then come and present your offering. Make*

friends quickly with your opponent at law while you are with him on the way, so that your opponent may not hand you over to the judge, and the judge to the officer, and you be thrown in prison.

The second Greek root word is 'synallassō' which means to negotiate or bargain with someone. Stephen uses this word in Acts 7:26 as he recounts the story of Moses' attempt to bring peace between two quarreling Hebrew brothers.

Acts 7:24-27 (NASB): *And when he [Moses] saw one of them being treated unjustly, he defended him and took vengeance for the oppressed by striking down the Egyptian. And he supposed that is brethren understood that God was granting them deliverance through him, but they did not understand. On the following day he appeared to them as they were fighting together, and he tried to reconcile them in peace, saying, "Men, you are brethren, why do you injure one another?" But the one who was injuring his*

neighbor pushed him away, saying, "WHO MADE
YOU A RULER AND JUDGE OVER US?

The third Greek root word is 'katallasso' which means to change, exchange, or be reconciled. This word is uniquely used only in the context of reconciliation of an individual with God or a wife with a husband.

> Romans 5:10 (NASB): *For if while we were enemies we were reconciled to God through the death of His Son, much more, having been reconciled, we shall be saved by His life.*

> 2 Corinthians 5:18-20 (NASB): *Now all these things are from God, who reconciled us to Himself through Christ and gave us the ministry of reconciliation, namely, that God was in Christ reconciling the world to Himself, not counting their trespasses against them, and He has committed to us the word of reconciliation.*

> *Therefore, we are ambassadors for Christ, as though God were making an appeal through us;*

we beg you on behalf of Christ, be reconciled to God.

1 Corinthians 7:10-11 (NASB): *But to the married I give instructions, not I, but the Lord, that the wife should not leave her husband (but if she does leave, she must remain unmarried, or else be reconciled to her husband), and that the husband should not divorce his wife.*

The fourth Greek root word is a form of the root above, 'apokatallassō,' which means to transfer from one state to another which is quite different, as to restore to favor. This word is used to express the work accomplished in Jesus' physical body, which includes the creation of one new man consisting of both Jew and Gentile by removing the dividing wall and reconciling all things to himself.

Ephesians 2:14-16 (NASB): *For He Himself is our peace, who made both groups into one and broke down the barrier of the dividing wall by abolishing in His flesh the enmity, which is the Law of commandments contained in ordinances, so that in Himself He might make the two into one new man, thus establishing peace, and might reconcile them both in one body to God through the cross, by it having put to death the enmity.*

Colossians 1:19-23 (NASB): *For it was the Father's good pleasure for all the fullness to dwell in Him, and through Him to reconcile all things to Himself, having made peace through the blood of His cross; through Him, I say, whether things on earth or things in heaven.*

And although you were formerly alienated and hostile in mind, engaged in evil deeds, yet He has now reconciled you in His fleshly body through death, in order to present you before Him holy and blameless and beyond reproach – if indeed you continue in the faith firmly established and steadfast, and not moved away from the hope of the gospel that you have heard, which was proclaimed in all creation under heaven, and of which I, Paul, was made a minister.

Since we have unpacked the distinctions between all the different 'reconciles' in the New Testament, let's connect the proper one to the 'ministry of reconciliation' we have been given in order to fully understand what that looks like.

The word 'reconciliation' is used only four times in the New Testament, and in all four instances the Greek word is 'katallagē' narrowing the connection to the exchange and return to favor associated with an individual being reconciled to God or a wife being reconciled to her husband (katallassō), and to the work Jesus accomplished in his physical body (apokatallassō). Two of the instances are in the 2 Corinthians 5 passage we looked at above. Romans 5:11 is the subsequent verse to Romans 5:10, which we looked at above. The final use is in Romans 11:15.

Romans 5:11 (NASB): *And not only this, but we also exult in God through our Lord Jesus Christ, through whom we have now received the reconciliation.*

Romans 11:13-15 (NASB): *But I am speaking to you who are Gentiles. Inasmuch then as I am an apostle of Gentiles, I magnify my ministry, if somehow I might move to jealousy my fellow countrymen and save some of them. For if their rejection is the reconciliation of the world, what will their acceptance be but life from the dead?*

So where does all of this leave us in understanding what 'reconciliation' means from God's perspective? Well, because the use is so narrow, we should unpack how God reconciles and how Jesus teaches about this specific activity of His Father to see what insights we can gain.

We know both from being taught, but even better by reading all the above scripture references for ourselves, the Father reconciles through the forgiveness established by His Son's death, burial, and resurrection, conquering death which is the penalty for sin. With this mechanism in place, the Father has a way to clear past records of wrong and restore us to a right relationship with Him.

Matthew 18:21-35 is Jesus' most detailed parable on how forgiveness in the Kingdom of God works. As we saw in the previous word, 'judgment,' we actually are those ones who choose the justice system under which our lives are evaluated. Likewise, we choose how forgiveness operates in our lives by how we engage in it toward others. As you will see, Jesus relies heavily on monetary and accounting systems as a way of explaining things in the Kingdom of God. We want to pay attention to this.

[Forgiveness] Then Peter came and said to Him, "Lord, how often shall my brother sin against me and I forgive him? Up to seven times?" Jesus said to him, "I do not say to you, up to seven times, but up to seventy times seven.

"For this reason the kingdom of heaven may be compared to a king who wished to settle accounts with his slaves. When he had begun to settle them, one who owed him ten thousand talents was brought to him. But since he did not

have the means to repay, his lord commanded him to be sold, along with his wife and children and all that he had, and repayment to be made. So the slave fell to the ground and prostrated himself before him, saying, 'Have patience with me and I will repay you everything.' And the lord of that slave felt compassion and released him and forgave him the debt. But that slave went out and found one of his fellow slaves who owed him a hundred denarii; and he seized him and began to choke him, saying, 'Pay back what you owe.' So his fellow slave fell to the ground and began to plead with him, saying, 'Have patience with me and I will repay you.' But he was unwilling and went and threw him in prison until he should pay back what was owed. So when his fellow slaves saw what had happened, they were deeply grieved and came and reported to their lord all that had happened. Then summoning him, his lord said to him, 'You wicked slave, I forgave you all that debt because you pleaded with me. Should you not also have had mercy on your fellow slave, in the same way that I had mercy on you?' And his lord, moved with anger, handed him over to the torturers until he should repay all that was owed him. My heavenly Father will also do the same to you, if each of you does not forgive his brother from your heart." (NASB)

From this parable about the Kingdom of God, it seems clear reconciliation is very much akin to reconciling accounting statements. The accounting terminology for writing a bad debt off the books is "the debt is forgiven." In this way, the balance is brought to zero. Nothing is owed. No obligation remains.

Have you ever experienced your brain keeping a record, like a tally sheet, of all the wrongs which have been done to you, or of all the good things you yourself have done? Our subconscious mind has a way of running a general ledger all the time. We have learned this from the lower law which operates in this world – the law of reciprocity. Much like the 'eye for an eye, tooth for a tooth' record-keeping law, this perpetual program runs in the background of our minds to exhaust the heart and hinder its ability to freely love.

The higher law of the Kingdom of God is the law of unconditionality (that's a made-up word). Forgiveness is always available to us for the asking. God's new mechanism, paid for by the blood of Jesus, brings our debt balance to zero every time we ask. He goes even further by His grace to supply blessings and favor in addition. He has given us that same ministry. We get to share the higher law of unconditionality and break the bonds of the law of reciprocity off of our lives and the lives of others. We demonstrate our true belief in the higher law by utilizing it in our relationships with others – we freely receive and freely give impartially. If we freely receive and do not freely give in kind, we are being partial to ourselves.

Practically, what does this look like? Does this mean that everything is rainbows and butterflies in relationships on the other side? No. Bringing an account balance to zero, you release others from your expectations, or holding them hostage by obligation to your standards, opinions, and requirements. You love them by honoring their free will, just as God does. You entrust people to the Lord and pray for His blessings in their lives. Reconciliation is the means of releasing others, which is the only way to give them the gift to freely choose if and how they want to be in relationship. By removing requirements to conform or comply with the traditions of man, reconciliation allows us to let go and love unconditionally.

Hear the difference between justice based on reciprocity and justice based on unconditionality:

> Hebrews 12:22-24 (AMPC): *But rather, you have come to Mount Zion, even to the city of the living God, the heavenly Jerusalem, and to countless multitudes of angels in festal gathering.*
>
> *And to the church (assembly) of the Firstborn who are registered [as citizens] in heaven, and to the God Who is Judge of all, and to the spirits of the righteous (the redeemed in heaven) who have been made perfect.*
>
> *And to Jesus, the Mediator (Go-between, Agent) of a new covenant, and to the sprinkled blood which speaks [of mercy], a better and nobler and more gracious message than the blood of Abel [which cried out for vengeance].*

I don't want to leave forgiveness without looking at Jesus' words when He first appears to His disciples after His resurrection.

> John 20:19-23 (NASB): *[Jesus among His Disciples] So when it was evening on that day, the first day of the week, and when the doors were shut where the disciples were, for fear of the Jews, Jesus came and stood in their midst and said to them, "Peace be with you." And when He had said this, He showed them both his hands and His side. The disciples then rejoiced when they saw the Lord. So Jesus said to them again, "Peace be with you; as the Father has sent Me, I also send you." And when He had said this, He breathed on them and said to them, "Receive the Holy Spirit. If you forgive the sins of any, their sins have been forgiven them; if you retain the sins of any, they have been retained."*

Notice how Jesus connects the Holy Spirit to peace and forgiveness.

So what does reconciliation in the Kingdom of God look like? How does this new definition, understanding the full meaning and accurate intention for the ministry of reconciliation He gave us, change your emotional responses to, your expectations about, and your efforts toward reconciliation in your life?

Jesus promises the Father's provision for everyone who seeks to live and rule with just and righteous judgments in His Kingdom.

> Matthew 6:31-33 (NASB): *Do not worry then, saying, 'What will we eat?' or 'What will we drink?' or 'What will we wear for clothing?' For the Gentiles eagerly seek all these things; for your heavenly Father knows that you need all these things. But seek first His kingdom and His righteousness, and all these things will be added to you.*

Provision seems to be a good word for us to consider next. Let's see what we can learn about it from God's perspective.

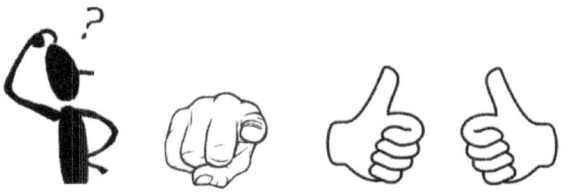

Provision

When you read the word 'provision,' what do you see? Do you see a cozy, white-picket fenced home overflowing with an abundance of possessions to satisfy every possible comfort, bountiful food and clothing, and a well-equipped garage with the requisite two cars?

When we look closely at passages in the Bible about God's promises to provide, we have to look at exactly what He is promising to provide. In Matthew 6, Jesus teaches his disciples much about the needs to make known to the Father, and how to make them known.

> Matthew 6:7-15, 31-33 (NASB): *"And when you are praying, do not use meaningless repetition as the Gentiles do, for they suppose that they will be heard for their many words. So do not be like them; for your Father knows what you need before you ask Him.*
>
> *"Pray, then, in this way:*
>
> *'Our Father who is in heaven,*
> *Hallowed by Your name.*
> *'Your kingdom come.*
> *Your will be done,*
> *On earth as it is in heaven.*
> *'Give us this day our daily bread.*
> *'And forgive us our debts, as we also have forgiven our debtors.*
> *'And do not lead us into temptation, but deliver*

us from evil. [For Yours is the kingdom and the power and the glory forever. Amen.]

For if you forgive others for their transgressions, your heavenly Father will also forgive you. But if you do not forgive others, then your Father will not forgive your transgressions. ...

Do not worry then, saying, 'What will we eat?' or 'What will we drink?' or 'What will we wear for clothing?' For the Gentiles eagerly seek all these things; for your heavenly Father knows that you need all these things. But seek first His kingdom and His righteousness, and all these things will be added to you.

Jesus instructs His disciples to pray for daily bread, forgiveness in accordance with how they have forgiven others, and freedom from temptation. He also assures them their basic needs of food, drink, and clothing will be met by the Father when they prioritize the Kingdom of God and His righteousness. His disciples are not to give any concern at all for these necessities.

As you study Jesus' life, His teachings, and the lives of the Apostles, it is evident everything needed for sustenance and to accomplish obedience to God's plan and purposes is also provided for those doing His will.

Matthew 21:1-3 (NASB): *[The Triumphal Entry] When they had approached Jerusalem and had come to Bethphage, at the Mount of Olives, then Jesus sent two disciples, say to them, "Go into the village opposite you, and immediately you will find a donkey tied there and a colt with her; untie them and bring them to Me. If anyone says anything to you, you shall say, 'The Lord has need of them,' and immediately he will send them."*

Mark 2:24-26 (NASB): *The Pharisees were saying to Him, "Look, why are they doing what is not lawful on the Sabbath?" And He said to them, "Have you never read what David did when he was in need and he and his companions became hungry; how he entered the house of God in the time of Abiathar the high priest, and ate the consecrated bread, which is not lawful for anyone to eat except the priests, and he also gave it to those who were with him?"*

Jesus met needs for physical healing and sustenance (Luke 9:11-17), but His ultimate purpose was to satisfy our need for forgiveness and freedom from the fear of death by providing eternal life in connection back to the Father.

The Father knows our eternal needs. His understanding of what we truly need goes far beyond what the world defines as our 'basic needs.' In the consumeristic world construct we exist in, the greatest marketers are those who can create a belief inside the minds of individuals that a 'want' is a 'need.' As soon as something is perceived to be a 'need,' then the very survival of that person depends on that 'need' being met. Listen to marketing for a few days. Do you hear and see it? Great marketers and advertisers employ sensory stimulus, psychology, and neuro-linguistic programming to appeal to the basic human need to belong. They tap into our preferences for ease, comfort, and pleasure to create a demand for material possessions as if they are basic survival necessities. The human subconscious which is convinced of this falsehood will not know how to be satisfied without these possessions because it fears not belonging or a life of drudgery and hard labor. It's all smoke and mirrors which never satisfies.

The Father knows we have become lost in these wants which are perceived as needs. He knows they keep us focused on the wrong things and cause us to miss what we need most. How often are we, with great repetition, crying out to Him for 'want-needs' when the basic needs He's promised to meet are indeed met and we don't notice or express gratitude? His silence to these cries is not punishment or indifference, but grace to break us free from a bottomless pit which will devour and never be satisfied, and also to drive us to a place of contentment. He is actually meeting a greater, more eternal need. We need the eyes to see His greater blessing.

1 Timothy 6:6 (NASB): *But godliness actually is a means of great gain when accompanied by contentment.*

Philippians 4:11-13 (NASB): *Not that I speak from want, for I have learned to be content in whatever circumstances I am. I know how to get along with humble means, and I also know how to live in prosperity; in any and every circumstance I have learned the secret of being filled and going hungry, both of having abundance and suffering need. I can do all things through Him who strengthens me.*

I am not endorsing a life of poverty by any means. God is a Father of abundance and generosity; He owns it all and can distribute it how He chooses. However, Jesus does admonish the practice of hoarding for security which needs no faith and provides a false security rooted in something which does not bring true assurance to our soul. And if our soul fears lack, or believes it to be a judgment, curse, or evidence of displeasure, we have not acquired the privilege of experiencing contentment by His strength in any and every circumstance. A fight against 'suffering need' gets in the way of our soul maturing to this level of contentment. The loving Father is likely to thwart such resistance to something much needed.

Luke 12:16-21, 33-34 (NASB): *And He [Jesus] told them a parable, saying, "The land of a rich man was very productive. And he began reasoning to himself, saying, 'What shall I do, since I have no place to store my crops?' Then he said, 'This is what I will do: I will tear down my barns and build larger ones, and there I will store all my grain and my goods. And I will say to my soul, "Soul, you have many goods laid up for many years to come; take your ease, eat, drink and be merry.'"" But God said to him, 'You fool! This very night your soul is required of you; and now who will own what you have prepared?' So is the man who stores up treasure for himself, and is not rich toward God."* ...

"Sell your possessions and give to charity; make yourselves money belts which do not wear out, an unfailing treasure in heaven, where no thief comes near nor moth destroys. For where your treasure is, there your heart will also be.

We clearly see God's priority in terms of meeting our needs is our soul. If every basic physical and emotional need were met without the soul prospering, the weightier matters from an eternal perspective would be neglected.

> 3 John 1:2 (NASB): *Beloved, I pray that in all respects you may prosper and be in good health, just as your soul prospers.*

Therefore, God's generosity has a purpose which is connected to what He is doing in our soul. One of the challenges in today's Christian culture is the belief that material possessions are a measure of God's favor, pleasure, and blessings toward an individual. Again, a subconscious mind convinced of this will evaluate themselves and everyone else according to that false measure. This creates another internal hoarding mechanism. Material possessions and praise of man are two of the greatest tests we will face on our spiritual journey toward maturity. How did the Apostles who walked and lived with Jesus, and the early church teach about and relate to their personal belongings and resources?

Acts 2:44-45 (NASB): *And all those who had believed were together and had all things in common; and they began selling their property and possessions and were sharing them with all, as anyone might have need.*

Acts 4:33-35 (NASB): *And with great power the apostles were giving testimony to the resurrection of the Lord Jesus, and abundant grace was upon them all. For there was not a needy person among them, for all who were owners of land or houses would sell them and bring the proceeds of the sales and lay them at the apostles' feet, and they would be distributed to each as any had need.*

2 Corinthians 8:12-15 (NASB): *For if the readiness [to give / share generously] is present, it is acceptable according to what a person has, not according to what he does not have. For this is not for the ease of others and for your affliction, but by way of equality – at this present time your abundance being a supply for their need, so that*

their abundance also may become a supply for your need, that there may be equality; as it is written, "HE WHO gathered MUCH DID NOT HAVE TOO MUCH, AND HE WHO gathered LITTLE HAD NO LACK."

Titus 3:14 (NASB): *Our people must also learn to engage in good deeds to meet pressing needs, so that they will not be unfruitful.*

1 John 3:17 (NASB): *But whoever has the world's goods, and sees his brother in need and closes his heart against him, how does the love of God abide in him?*

The Lord Jesus Christ is the storehouse from which God the Father supplies all our needs – according to His order and priorities and not our mis-labled 'want-needs.'

Colossians 2:1-3 (NASB): *[You Are Built Up in Christ] For I want you to know how great a struggle I have on your behalf and for those who are at Laodicea, and for all those who have not personally seen my face, that their hearts may be encouraged, having been knit together in love, and attaining to all the wealth that comes from the full assurance of understanding, resulting in a true knowledge of God's mystery, that is, Christ Himself, in who are hidden all the treasures of wisdom and knowledge.*

Hebrews 4:15-16 (NASB): *For we do not have a high priest who cannot sympathize with our weaknesses, but One who has been tempted in all things as we are, yet without sin. Therefore let us draw near with confidence to the throne of grace, so that we may receive mercy and find grace to help in time of need.*

Philippians 4:19 (NASB): *And my God will supply all your needs according to His riches in glory in Christ Jesus.*

So what does provision in the Kingdom of God look like? How does this new definition, understanding the full meaning and accurate intention of God's provision for and in our lives, change your emotional responses to what you have in your life?

He has enough who is content

WANTS
Things we don't really need but would like to have.

NEEDS
Things we must have in order to stay alive.

water

NEEDS
must have to
live.

food

shelter
(home)

clothing

DAILY BREAD

שָׁלוֹם
SHALOM
peace, safety, quiet, tranquility, contentment

◈ Satisfied, moderation, sufficient, enough.

◈ The opposite of covetousness or being dissatisfied.

◈ An attitude of mind. How you view your current state of affair!

FINDING CONTENTMENT

Proverbs 30:7-9 (NASB):

Two things I asked of You,
Do not refuse me before I die:
Keep deception and lies far from me,
Give me neither poverty nor riches;
Feed me with the food that is my portion,
That I not be full and deny You and say, "Who is
the LORD?"
Or that I not be in want and steal,
And profane the name of my God.

What a wonderful request! Such wisdom leads to a life of contentment and rest. How genius of the Lord to conclude this study of words with *that* word – rest. Let's go there now.

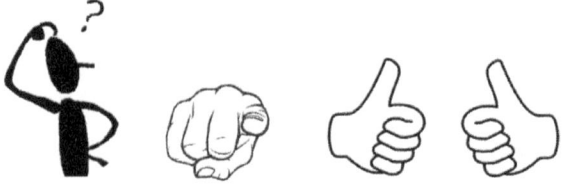

Rest

When you read the word 'rest,' what do you see? Do you see vacations on the beach, cuddling on the couch with a book or to watch TV, a relaxing soak in the tub, a day in the park, a good dream-filled sleep, or a forced physical recovery?

Do you feel it is necessary for you to escape your life in some form or fashion in order to rest? Rest is a major theme in God's Word. Rest shows up for the first time in the thirty-third verse of the Bible – Genesis 2:2. Right from the beginning, God included His very own rest as part of the pattern of life for His creation. We know God does not get weary, nor does He sleep, so what exactly is His rest and why did He rest at the conclusion of His creative work?

Isaiah 40:28 (NASB): *Do you not know? Have you not heard? The Everlasting God, the Lord, the Creator of the ends of the earth Does not become weary or tired. His understanding is inscrutable.*

Psalm 121:3-4 (NASB):

He will not allow your foot to slip;
He who keeps you will not slumber.
Behold, He who keeps Israel
Will neither slumber nor sleep.

Though God does not require rest, we, His creation, do. We are weak in our nature, and apart from rest being demonstrated for His newly created children, we would have had no understanding of it. Therefore, though God Himself didn't require it, He modeled it for human understanding so we would know how to practice it. 'Rest' as a standalone word apart from example carries no meaningful definition.

How reassuring it is to have a God as Father Who is so concerned for our well-being that He will step into something He *does not need* for the benefit of our comprehension, knowing *we do need it!* Equally reassuring is the truth He does not need it, so will never tire in His availability and goodness toward us.

Lest we think our requirement for rest is strictly physical in nature, let's understand God's meaning and benefit of rest more fully.

The fullest Hebrew meaning of rest is communicated in the Shabbat liturgy: "a rest of love freely given, a rest of truth and sincerity, a rest in peace and tranquility, in quietude and safety." Rest is yoked in the same breath to holiness. The cessation from toiling makes room for God-awareness and God's activity. All of our activity obscures the glory of God from our perception. If we won't stop ourselves, we won't make space for God to be God in our lives and our world. We are far too busy creating names, reputations, security, and storehouses for ourselves to receive the inheritance He has established and set aside for us.

Psalm 46:10 (NASB): *"Cease striving and know that I am God; I will be exalted among the nations, I will be exalted in the earth."*

Isaiah 30:15-16 (NASB): *For thus the Lord, GOD, the Holy One of Israel, has said,*

"In repentance and rest you will be saved,
In quietness and trust is your strength."
But you were not willing,
And you said, "No, for we will flee on horses,"
Therefore you shall flee!
"And we will ride on swift horses,"
Therefore those who pursue you shall be swift.

Generation after generation, humankind demonstrated their zeal for going after things their own way, preventing sustainable exhibits of God's desired activity in the earth for the benefit of His creation. By the time of Moses, God must give His chosen people a literal command as part of their holy covenant to Him to make a way for Him to demonstrate His work instead of theirs, intended as a light and easy yoke. Interestingly, God's heart wants to provide everything we require, making life simple and peaceful, but disallows any credit being taken for our own efforts. What does that say about our nature?

In the New Testament, this command is revealed as a promise and gift we can choose to receive. The Greek word for rest (repose) is katapausis and it occurs only nine times in the New Testament. Katapausis means the act of giving rest; a state of settled or final rest, a place of rest, place of abode, dwelling, habitation. Jesus is our demonstration of living a life of rest in a world where He assures us we will have tribulations (John 16:33). The first New Testament occurrence of katapausis is a reference to Isaiah 66:1-2 of God Himself speaking.

Acts 7:49 (NASB):

'HEAVEN IS MY THRONE,
AND EARTH IS THE FOOTSTOOL OF MY FEET;
WHAT KIND OF HOUSE WILL YOU BUILD FOR ME?'
says the Lord,
'OR WHAT PLACE IS THERE FOR MY REPOSE?

All remaining eight occurrences of katapausis are in Hebrews 3 and 4 – the great dissertation on God's promised rest.

Hebrews 3:5-18 (NASB): *Now Moses was faithful in all His house as a servant, for a testimony of those things which were to be spoken later; but Christ was faithful as a Son over His house – whose house we are, if we hold fast our confidence and the boast of our hope firm until the end.*

Therefore, just as the Holy Spirit says,

"TODAY IF YOU HEAR HIS VOICE,
DO NOT HARDEN YOUR HEARTS AS WHEN THEY PROVOKED ME,

AS IN THE DAY OF TRIAL IN THE WILDERNESS,
WHERE YOUR FATHERS TRIED Me BY TESTING Me,
AND SAW MY WORKS FOR FORTY YEARS.
"THEREFORE I WAS ANGRY WITH THIS
GENERATION,
AND SAID, 'THEY ALWAYS GO ASTRAY IN THEIR
HEART,
AND THEY DID NOT KNOW MY WAYS';
AS I SWORE IN MY WRATH,
'THEY SHALL NOT ENTER MY REST.'"

[The Peril of Unbelief] Take care, brethren, that there not be in any one of you an evil, unbelieving heart that falls away from the living God. But encourage one another day after day, as long as it is still called "Today," so that none of you will be hardened by the deceitfulness of sin. For we have become partakers of Christ, if we hold fast the beginning of our assurance firm until the end, while it is said,

"TODAY IF YOU HEAR HIS VOICE,
DO NOT HARDEN YOUR HEARTS, AS WHEN THEY
PROVOKED ME."

For who provoked Him when they had heard? Indeed, did not all those who came out of Egypt led by Moses? And with whom was He angry for forty years? Was it not with those who sinned, whose bodies fell in the wilderness? And to whom did He swear that they would not enter His rest, but to those who were disobedient? So we see that they were not able to enter because of unbelief.

This passage in Hebrews 3 clearly connects an inability to enter God's rest to an unbelieving heart (sin) which is disobedient. Think about that. Complete rest is available for a heart which is so deeply rooted in a belief in God's love and goodness that it will obey whatever He asks of it. Jesus lived precisely like this. Unbelief is sin which is demonstrated in disobedience with no rest. Belief is faith (righteousness) demonstrated in obedience with complete rest in God's goodness regardless of outward results of that obedience. We do not measure the results. We measure how obedient we are. Rest is in obedience firmly rooted and established on the belief in God's holy nature and essence of love. In John 10:27, Jesus states clearly that His sheep, those of His pasture, hear His voice and follow Him. That is the premise of rest established by obedience.

Hebrews 4:1-11 (NASB): *[The Believer's Rest] Therefore, let us fear if, while a promise remains of entering His rest, any one of you may seem to have come short of it. For indeed we have had good news preached to us, just as they also; but the word they heard did not profit them, because it was not united by faith in those who heard. For we who have believed enter that rest, just as He has said,*

"AS I SWORE IN MY WRATH,
THEY SHALL NOT ENTER MY REST,"

Although His works were finished from the foundation of the world. For He has said somewhere concerning the seventh day: "AND GOD RESTED ON THE SEVENTH DAY FROM ALL HIS WORKS"; and again in this passage, "THEY SHALL NOT ENTER MY REST." Therefore, since it remains for some to enter it, and those who formerly had good news preached to them failed to enter because of disobedience, He again fixes a certain day, "Today," saying through David after so long a time just as has been said before,

"TODAY IF YOU HEAR HIS VOICE,
DO NOT HARDEN YOUR HEARTS."

For if Joshua had given them rest, He would not have spoken of another day after that. So there remains a Sabbath rest for the people of God. For the one who has entered His rest has himself also rested from his works, as God did from His. Therefore let us be diligent to enter that rest, so that no one will fall, through following the same example of disobedience.

The beginning of every new day is 'Today' offering a fresh opportunity to listen to His voice and obey. The basis of obedience is faith in the love and goodness of Our Father in heaven. Obedience rooted in fear is not established in perfected love.

1 John 4:18 (NASB): *There is no fear in love; but perfect love casts out fear, because fear involves punishment, and the one who fears is not perfected in love.*

One of the ways the Lord teaches me is through the use of acrostics. I was taking a long walk along the river one day in 2010 when He began teaching me about rest. I heard Him simply saying the word over and over, and I waited for what He wanted to speak about it. He said R-E-S-T is Receiving Everlasting Salvation and Truth. Salvation is the beginning of rest, but receiving the fullness of truth is its culmination. True to God's way, it's a paradox that entering His rest requires us to be diligent, to labor, and to strive.

So what does God's rest look like? How does this new definition, understanding the full meaning and accurate intention of His rest for our lives, change your moment-by-moment interpretation and emotional responses to events in your life?

1 John 4:16-17 (NASB): *We have come to know and have believed the love which God has for us. God is love, and the one who abides in love abides in God, and God abides in him. By this, love is perfected with us, so that we may have confidence in the day of judgment; because as He is, so also we are in this world.*

John 17:22-24 (NASB): *[Their Future Glory] The glory which You have given Me I have given to them, that they may be one, just as We are one; I in them and You in Me, that they may be perfected in unity, so that the world may know that You sent Me, and loved them, even as You have loved Me. Father, I desire that they also, whom You have given Me, be with Me where I am, so that they may see My glory which You have given Me, for you loved Me before the foundation of the world.*

ABOUT THE AUTHOR

Tricia Kaye Exman is a transformation coach, leadership developer, author, and speaker who is passionate about celebrating authentic lives, honoring individual stories, and focusing on eternity. Whether coaching, writing, speaking, or creating personal development content and tools, Tricia is focused on inviting and guiding people into recovering all the intended possibilities for their life. You can learn more at triciaexman.com and coachexman.com

Tricia's Other Works

Twisted Truths:
Three Things That Thwart Transformation

YADA, YADA, YADA...
Why Should I Follow Jesus?

Ask Yourself JUMBO Journal:
303 Questions for Personal Discovery & Growth

Spirit-to-Spirit:
A Collection of Articles from the Presence of The LORD

"Show up and Shine"

Pioneering Expeditions into
Fearless,
Brilliant,
Limitless Living!

ThePresenceCoach.com

You Have One Life!
Live It Expansively!

Join a Limitless Living Group!
Life-Changing Community
Develop and Expand Networks
Convenience and Affordability
Certified Life Strategists

276

Your life is busy!

MyGoCoach coaches your busy life
as you go to help you accomplish the things you want
with the time you have!

Set Goals.
Work on Habits.
Be Inspired.
Learn.
Grow.

What's Your Next Best Step?
Take It!

FREE Download exclusively from
Presence Coaching!

MyGoCoach.com

Made in United States
North Haven, CT
09 August 2022

22457902R00157